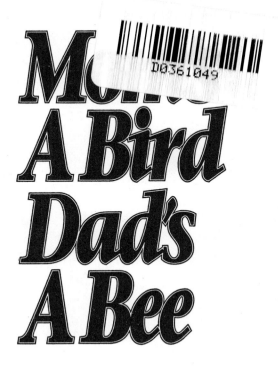

Mom's A Bird Dad's A Bee

MARY ANN MAYO

HARVEST HOUSE PUBLISHERS
Eugene, Oregon 97402

Except where otherwise indicated, all Scripture verses are taken from the Holy Bible, New International Version, Copyright © 1973, 1978, 1984 by the International Bible Society. Used by permission of Zondervan Bible Publishers.

Illustrations from Stephen A. Grunlan, *Marriage and the Family: A Christian Perspective (Zondervan)*.

To Joe, Joey, and Malika

Special thanks for the prayers of Janell and the Thursday morning group. Acknowledgment is also due Alice Harned, Kin Millen, Jim Ruark, Kathy Heetderks, and Lela Gilbert for their efforts on my behalf. Thank you.

MOM'S A BIRD, DAD'S A BEE

Copyright © 1991 by Harvest House Publishers
Eugene, Oregon 97402

ISBN 0-89081-825-8

Printed in the United States of America.

91-16400

Contents

Introduction

PART ONE: You and "The Facts"

PART TWO: Your Child and "The Facts"

PART THREE: Special Issues of Sex Education

If you would like Dr. and Mrs. Mayo to come to your community to present a seminar on communicating with your children about a values approach to sexuality, they can be contacted at:

REFERENCE POINT
Box 8022
Redlands, CA 92375

The seminar is titled:

DECENT DISCLOSURE
Raising morally responsible children
in an irresponsible world.
Questions and answers about sex
for children from birth to puberty.

Introduction

A Surprise Attack of the Birds and the Bees

Two-year-old Tamara and four-year-old Austin were engrossed in play in Tamara's bedroom. Jenny, their mother, was grateful for the few minutes of quiet which allowed her to set the table and prepare the evening meal. As she worked at the sink peeling carrots, Jenny reviewed the activities of the day, savoring the luxurious moments of uninterrupted thought. Little voices making their way up the hallway signaled that her luxury was soon to be over. She turned to see a pretty good imitation of a two-year-old pregnant lady shuffling into the kitchen. Austin was right behind her.

"Okay, Tamara, just be careful," said Austin to his sister with all the concern of an expectant father. Then he looked up at Jenny and announced solemnly, "Mom, we're playing mom and dad. I'm taking Tamara to the hospital to have a baby." Tamara, never one to do anything halfheartedly, emoted appropriately and clung to the soon-to-be-delivered baby doll they had stuffed under her "Precious Moments" T-shirt.

Jenny smiled. "That's wonderful, kids. When your little baby is born, I sure would like to see him or her."

"Oh, we already know it's a her, Mom," Austin assured smugly. "We had 'extra-sound.' "

"Yeah, Mom, it's *really* a girl," chimed in Tamara as she pulled up her shirt and touched the baby doll's crotch. "See, no 'peanuts,' just a 'bajina,'!"

Jenny put her hand on her mouth to stifle a laugh that might have dimmed the "proud parents' " moment of glory. But as the children hurried off to the "hospital" in the family room, she couldn't help but wonder about the scene they had just played for her. *Where did they get their script? Have Chuck and I talked about pregnancy around them? Are they hearing about sex from Grandma and Grandpa or their friends? Is Austin getting indoctrinated on subjects like penises, vaginas, and ultrasound in preschool and passing it on to Tamara?*

5

Did "Sesame Street" slip in a unit on sex education when I wasn't looking?

Jenny's amusement at her children suddenly turned to thoughtful concern tinged with anxiety. *What more do they know about sex?* she mused. *What should they know about it at their ages? And when and how are we supposed to tell them about "the birds and the bees"?* Jenny sighed as she loaded the food processor with carrots and flipped the switch. "Wow, do Chuck and I have ever have something to talk about tonight!" she mumbled beneath the whir of the blades.

Like Jenny and Chuck, every parent alive desires to do the best job possible at raising his or her children, including teaching them about sex. The hard part is making it happen! When sex education is the issue, parental intentions are usually good. But chances are that more information will be conveyed through the parents' unconscious example—good and bad—than through a well-thought out program of parent-to-child instruction. And the more parents waffle on their responsibility to supply factual, timely sex education, the more vulnerable their children become to input from an ever-widening variety of unknown or unreliable sources. Yet most parents smoke-screen their way through the subject with vague generalities or painful silence *because they just don't know what to say.*

Wouldn't you like to break that long-running, traditional cycle of silence with your children? Wouldn't it be wonderful to answer their inquiries about where babies come from without your heart hitting the floor? When they ask, "Where did I come from?" wouldn't it be nice to be calm enough to check out if they mean Minneapolis before you bore them with a two-hour illustrated lecture on human anatomy? Wouldn't it be great to feel confident that you are no longer perpetuating myths and half-truths about sex but really communicating healthy, correct information and clearly sharing your moral value system? If that sounds good to you, read on. This book is for you.

But I can hear rumblings from others of you: "Who are you trying to kid? There's no way I could ever talk to my children about sex, let alone do it calmly. I'll just pass on the misinformation I received. Or better yet, I'll do what most folks do: I won't say anything! Somehow I've muddled through on next to nothing; my kids will too."

If that's your response, I invite you to keep reading also, because you can't get off the hook that easily. Please absorb the basic premise of this book: _You are now and always will be the greatest influence on your child's developing sexuality._ You may try to deny your responsibility, or you may try to extricate yourself from it, but you can't escape it. If you don't teach your kids about sex, somebody else will, and that somebody may give them the wrong information in the wrong setting at the wrong time. I believe that even the most repressed or apprehensive parent (yes, even you!) can and must take the lead in teaching his or her children about sex. This book was written to show you how you can do it confidently.

There are two important elements to your influence on your child's sexuality: your example and your words. The most powerful of the two is your example of sexual attitudes and actions. Your example, not your words, will create the atmosphere of sexuality in your home. No matter what you say, your children will learn more about sex through what you do.

That's why Part One of this book deals with your sexual attitudes and actions. Before we get into the important strategies of how to talk with your children about sex, you need to understand your own view and expression of sexuality.

Your attitudes about sex have been impacted by your background and upbringing. What you were taught about sex, and how sexuality was modeled by your parents and other significant adults, has a large bearing on your attitudes toward sexuality today and how well-prepared you feel to teach your children about sex. In Chapter 1 we will talk about your past sexual influences and their impact on your present attitudes and practices.

The culture in which we live has also influenced your sexual attitudes and behavior. Parents and children alike are bombarded daily by the messages of a permissive society to be sexual, sensual, and seductive. We are commanded by God not to be *of* the world, but we are stuck *in* the world, and the world's idea of sexuality, which is very different from God's idea, makes insidious inroads into our lives. In Chapters 2 and 3 we will contrast the world's view of sex with God's view in order to clearly understand how we should think and behave sexually as adults, and how we should teach our children to think and behave.

A major element of the sex-education-by-example of your children is your relationship with your husband or wife. No, I'm not talking about inviting the kids into your bedroom for live demonstrations. I'm saying that if your sexuality as a couple, including what you do in public as well as in private, is marked by love, respect, and caring, your kids will have a healthy picture of what it means for man and woman to love each other. But if your sexual relationship is characterized by selfishness and disrespect, your kids will pick it up, and it will affect their concept of sex and sexuality. In Chapters 4 and 5 we will focus on the sexual systems of the woman and the man respectively, including a review of basic reproductive anatomy.

The second important element of your influence on your child's sexuality is your words—what you tell them about sex. That's what Part Two is all about. There are two basic considerations for telling your children about sex. The first is the facts. If you're going to teach them something, you'd better know the material: the pieces and parts, their correct names, and their functions. The second consideration is timing: which facts should be discussed at which stage of the child's development. In Part Two we'll talk about facts and timing together as we consider sex education at four age-levels: the preschool child, the school-aged child, the adolescent, and the young single. And since a child's inquisitiveness is a key to the timeliness of some facts, each chapter of age level description concludes with questions which are typical to children in that age group and sample responses to help you think about how you will respond to similar questions.

There are a number of special issues relating to sex education which require separate treatment. In Part Three we'll consider several of them: sex education in the schools, the sex education of the disabled child, sexual abuse and molestation, and four especially hot issues impacting sex education— homosexuality, masturbation, abortion, and contraception.

I hope your goal in reading this book is not simply to load up with all the right answers. That's an unreachable goal anyway, because your quick-thinking children will no doubt come up with a few questions that neither you nor I have thought about before! Let me suggest a more realistic goal: that you become an approachable, "askable" parent who can demonstrate and verbalize biblical values about sex effectively to your children. I have worked with hundreds of parents just like you who have reached this goal. Be encouraged; you can do it too!

PART 1

Getting
the Facts
on
"The Facts"

1

What Is Sex to You?

Human life is a sexual experience from day one. Despite the common notion that children are sexually dormant until their teens, even a newborn's world is one of sensuous delight and sexual stimulation. His mother's body is the immediate source of an orgy of gastronomical and tactile satisfactions. She floods his sense of smell, taste, and sight (a newborn locks onto his mother's face shortly after birth and the visual bonding experience begins). Even from before birth his sense of hearing is tuned into her heartbeat and voice.

But most of all, he responds to her touch. Our skin is our largest and most sensitive sex organ. Children whose need for touch is not met fail to develop in a normal way physically and mentally. Most tragically, they are unable to establish close bonds with others. The more we learn about newborns, the more we realize how vital proper physical touch is to healthy development.

Not only is a newborn's sensory apparatus in operation, so is his sexual apparatus. Fifty percent of little boy babies have an erection before the umbilical cord is cut. Little girl babies will lubricate within four hours of birth. Lubrication for females and erection for males is the first sign of sexual arousal. No one slipped *Playboy* or *Playgirl* into the delivery room of these sensuous little creatures! They are merely doing what comes naturally.

The ability of our sexual system to respond is with us from birth. And barring physical disability, the system will still be operating until the day we die—whatever the age. All healthy people respond sexually throughout life. Men have innumerable erections during sleep. They often awake with an erection, mistakenly blamed on the need to urinate, a natural assumption after eight hours in bed. Women lubricate throughout the night. In other words, without putting much energy into it, we're pretty sexual creatures.

"But what about old Aunt Emma?" you say. "There's no way she..." Surprise! Aunt Emma, Grandpa Roscoe, and even celibate Father O'Hara down at the Catholic church are sexually responsive too. They may not choose to be sexually *active,* but their sexual response systems keep trucking right along because that's how God made them.

Sex for a Lifetime

Lifetime sexuality is a fact of life. As children we are tuned in to our bodies. It's only as we grow up that we become so deplorably unaware of our sensuous selves. My husband and I always tell our counseling clients that our task is to make them as aware of their bodies as they were at two years old.

The ability to respond sexually is always with us, just as with all other natural physical responses. But just as with other physical responses, sexual response can be ignored or repressed. Since sexual response is a normal bodily function (as are respiration, circulation, sleep, defecation, urination, hunger, and thirst), anything that affects the other body systems can affect the ability to respond sexually. Stress, for example, may prompt you to raid the refrigerator or lose your appetite, sleep all day or walk the floor at night, increase your desire for sex or decrease it. No one can tell you exactly how you will react physically or sexually to stress, fatigue, depression, illness, etc.—but you will react.

But before you run to Masters and Johnson, Phil Donahue, or *Redbook* for a solution to your sexual "problem," take a few moments to absorb a concept that may be very different from what you grew up with: *Sexual responsiveness is a natural function of your body.* Sex should fit within the framework of the totality of our lives. We shouldn't draw extra attention to it with red flags or hide it under the rug. It's as important and unimportant as any other part of life. Just think: You can finally let go of the mistaken concept that your sexual urges came upon you when the devil entered your body after that dance in ninth grade! Whew, what a relief!

God and the Facts of Life

However, while sexual responsiveness is simply one of many natural, God-designed physical functions, many consider sex a necessary evil of life. It's this misunderstanding and subsequent misuse of sex that cause our sexual difficulties. Our sexuality and sensuality are gifts from God. Remember, on the seventh day God reviewed His world and determined "it was very good" (Genesis 1:31). "It" includes your ability to experience passion, to feel good physically, and to enjoy sexual delight with your mate.

In his book *Sex for Christians,* Lewis Smedes speaks of us as "body-persons." God could have made us spirits without bodies. He could have made us asexual. But He made us body-persons and called what He made "very good." Furthermore, God did not send a fireball to earth when He wanted to reveal Himself. He sent a real, live body-person: our Lord Jesus. As Smedes points out, our problem with being body-persons is discerning what is of the world and what is of God. We'll explore that topic in greater detail in Chapters 2 and 3.

The Facts of Life in Your Life

Sex is special, different from anything else. Poets have written of its power and mystery. Pagan religions have used it in their highest forms of worship. The Arabs refer to sex as "the great equalizer." No matter what a man or woman's station in life may be, the joys of sex are available to him or her.

Sex is a natural phenomenon and more: complicated, profound, and forever mysterious. But what is sex to you? Before you embark on a campaign to educate your children about their sexuality, make sure you are cognizant of your attitudes and feelings. You don't need to be totally free from sexual problems to be an effective teacher, but you must be aware of the areas in which you are prejudiced, unclear, or hurting. Awareness will help you prevent perpetuating your frustrations, hurts, and prejudicial views in the vulnerable and impressionable minds of your children.

Sexuality in Your History

Through my teaching and counseling I've discovered a little tool that seems to help most people explore their sexual attitudes and mentally prepare to be effective communicators with their children. Identifying and evaluating your childhood feelings about your sexual identity and experiences will give you important clues to your present attitudes and behavior regarding your sexuality. I urge you to pause here and think about the following questions, then discuss them with your spouse:

1. What do you recall your parents and other relatives saying about your being born? Were their comments positive or negative? Were you what your parents wanted?

2. Did you have sufficient opportunities as a child to be around the opposite sex? the same sex? What male and female images have you incorporated from those experiences?

3. Did your father respect women and treat them accordingly? Did your mother respect men and treat them accordingly? What attitudes have you incorporated from your parents' treatment of the opposite sex?

4. What were you told about your sexual curiosity as a child? Were the remarks rational? threatening? destructive? positive? indulgent?

5. Was the subject of sex ignored in your home? If so, how did you feel about that?

6. What terms did your parents use for your sex organs? How did you learn "the facts of life"?

7. Were you taught how to protect yourself sexually? Did your parents or guardians fail to protect you sexually? Were you abused sexually? Did your parents or guardians try to arouse you sexually with stories or actions?

8. What is your primary feeling about your body? about your sex organs?

9. Recall a sexual experience you had as a child. What feelings well up inside you about that experience?

10. What defense mechanisms did you create to deal with your childhood sexual self?

11. What are your feelings about the opposite sex today?

12. At your age and stage of life, what do you consider to be appropriate sexual behavior? Do facts and logic support your conclusions?

13. If you are at an appropriate stage for an intimate partner, evaluate your sexual interactions. Are they adequate? joyful? frustrating? exploitative? mutually satisfying? something else?

14. Do you have adequate information about your sexuality and that of the opposite sex? If not, gather more data by reading, attending classes, or talking to professionals.

15. If you have a problem with sex, is there something you can do about it you haven't done yet? Do you need to see a counselor? Have you had a physical exam? Do you need to take a vacation from work? rearrange some of your environment? something else?

Incidentally, if your parents failed to provide you with adequate information on sex and sexuality, don't be too hard on them. After all, sexual research was taboo until about the last 30 years, and the most serious research has only occurred in the last 20 years. Your parents' "facts" were probably about as accurate as Aunt Ada's chocolate cake recipe: a pinch of this, a tad of that. They didn't know all the facts; there's no way they could have.

So there's no reason to burden yourself or them with recriminations for the bad trips they laid on you. They likely did the best they could with what they had. If you're angry with them about it, let it go. On the other hand, you can't use their failure as an excuse for your ignorance. The research has been done and is readily available to you.

Further Preparation Needed?

All right, you have given serious thought to the questions. You and your spouse have even gone over them together, and you have pinpointed some areas of concern as well as developed some insight into the way you learned about sex. Now what?

For some of you, this insight and the information you receive from the following chapters will give you the confidence and the material you need to get the ball rolling with your children. But if you are not yet comfortable with your sexuality for some reason, here are a few suggestions.

Counseling. If your problem seems deeply rooted in your past, don't hesitate to seek help from a competent professional. Whatever you do, don't just ask a friend. Chances are they know less than you do. Our sexual selves are too important and complex to be toyed with by amateurs. Go to someone who has training in counseling and sexuality. Besides, if your sexual history and information involves another person such as your spouse, it would be a breach of trust to tell a friend. If your problem centers around your relationship with your spouse, a good counselor will want to see you both.

Seminars and support groups. There are a number of seminars around that help parents and teachers break through their inhibitions of talking about sex. It's not unusual for people to be knowledgeable on the subject and yet experience great difficulty verbalizing the knowledge they have. These seminars often take this into account by providing role-playing experiences for the participants.

Some groups that I've been involved with made up questions that children of various ages and both sexes might ask.

For example, a two- to four-year-old girl might want to know, "Why does Johnny have a penis and I don't?" A member of the group answers the question aloud with vocabulary appropriate for the age level. If another member feels he can contribute something more or answer in a different way, he is encouraged to do so. Participants are able to learn from one another during the role-play. As the role-play continues, participants generally find their comfort level and ability to think on their feet increasing.

Of course, this exercise is nothing more than desensitization. Most of us have been raised in a world that rarely included verbalizing the proper names for our body parts. (That's right, you can no longer use "wee-wee" for penis!) Desensitization is a necessary exercise for many parents.

A wonderful discussion icebreaker involves having mixed groups draw the male and female sexual systems. This exercise stimulates a great deal of discussion about just what a sexual system is. (It's *not* just the reproductive system, but that's what most people will draw.) Often this exercise provides a first-time opportunity for many parents to discuss sexual matters in mixed company.

The resulting drawings, sometimes enhanced by balloons, pipe cleaners, Saran Wrap, polished rocks, and so on, are a delight to share and a wonderful teaching device. Comparing the creative efforts of different groups enables the facilitator to make educational observations and corrections in a non-threatening way.

There have been times when I have desensitized groups by having them sing the names of body parts, including some of our more colorful terms for them. But I suggest that you do this only if the windows are closed and Aunt Emma isn't visiting!

It's possible that you could organize such a seminar or sharing group through your church, PTA, or a group of friends. You need a "resident expert"—a physician or a nurse to keep the facts straight. But you should be able to handle the rest of the preparations with ease.

Sex education classes for parents. If your local school district provides sex education courses for students, you may find that portions of it are open to parents. For example, the Roman Catholic schools of St. Paul and Minneapolis, Minnesota, offer their sex education course to parents first. When the students take the course, they are encouraged to grill their folks as part of their homework. Contact your local school district for courses which may be available to you.

Is Enough Ever Enough?

You may be saying, "Even if I came to terms with my sexuality and learned all I could about sex, I'm afraid my kids will ask questions I won't know how to answer. I don't think I'll ever be really prepared to talk to my kids about sex."

Any good teacher will tell you she never tries to fool a kid when she doesn't know the answer. Even when you have prepared thoroughly, situations and questions will arise for which you don't have an answer or need some time to think. It's just fine to say, "I don't know the answer to that; let's look it up together" or "I'll have to think about that and get back to you." In doing so you prove that you are human (which, by the way, your child already knows!), and you are providing a positive model for problem-solving.

Jesus, the Master Teacher, provides plenty of support for us in this honest approach to educating our children. We are reminded in Scripture through His parables and example to pray, think, and act. This plan works just as well for sex education as for anything else.

2

You're in the World but You Don't Have to Be of It

Hi, Joe. Thanks for seeing me today. I've got a great idea for you." Ben bounced into Joe's office full of life. He wanted to look like a winner. His last concept for a sitcom had bombed. Whatever made him think a show built around a traditional family would go over anyway? *I'm lucky to get another shot*, he thought as he sat down opposite the network executive.

"Hello, Ben. Great idea, you say? It better beat that last bummer you brought in. Got to keep those ratings up." Joe knew where the bottom line was. He didn't have time to mess around.

"This baby is guaranteed to please," Ben began. "Imagine this, Joe: a family that's a family in name only. Everyone fights, no one has respect for Dad, the kids are smart-mouths, and Mom is a master at put-downs!"

"I love it, Ben!" Joe roared enthusiastically. "In fact, I love it so much that I'm going to do two sitcoms in the same format, one of them a cartoon. They'll be number one and two in the ratings. Way to go, Ben. The American public is going to love you for this."

The Worldly Facts of Life

Well, the conversation didn't go exactly that way. But the shows did. The 1990 Neilsen ratings indicated that TV programs featuring bickering families with distorted sex roles were hits with the 18-to-24-year-old age group.[1] The number one show, and the primary model of family life for America's impressionable young adults, was "The Simpsons"—five very dysfunctional, near-ghoulish creatures whose life together is indeed a cartoon of the real thing. Number two, "Roseanne," and number seven, "Married with Children," are flesh-and-blood versions of the same model.

Number six, "The Cosby Show," portrays a family that loves, communicates, and has fun. However, they do so without any reference to a spiritual dimension to life, with parents who never seem to get stressed out by their work, and with kids who get feisty but always listen to reason. The number three show, "Cheers," centers around a group of characters who become a "family" as the staff and regular patrons of a bar. The show welcomed its new female lead with a year-long story line about who would bed her first, with the obviously experienced male lead scheming week after week for the "honor."

True, by the time you read this some of these shows may be relegated to daytime reruns while new ones occupy Neilsen's top ten. But I'm afraid negative family values will continue to be a long-running prime-time feature on our TV screens.

Sex in the Media

Television is just one example of how our attitudes about sex, marriage, and family life are continually being influenced by the secular world in general and the media in particular. Daytime programming is flooded with soap operas where monogamous, lifetime relationships and legitimate births are the exception, not the rule. The movies shown both on regular TV and cable at all hours of the day and night glamorize illicit sex, homosexuality, and sexual deviations and abuses most of our parents never heard of.

Advertising, both electronic and print, is another example of how the world entices us and our children to "be sexual and act sexually or miss out." Ads like those showing cherubs in brand-name designer jeans rush our children to grow up and taste a world they only think they are prepared for. When my daughter was a little girl, she loved black clothes, but we could never find anything for her in black. Then as now, dressing in black was associated with being grown-up and sexy. Today, thanks to Madison Avenue, black is only one of a number of sexually provocative aspects of children's clothing.

Growing Up Too Soon

Another complication to childhood sexuality exists in our world which didn't exist a generation ago. Our kids eat better food, take more vitamins and minerals, and are exposed to better immunization and medical care than their parents or grandparents. As a result they mature physically earlier than any generation in history. In the 1800s the mean age of the onset of menstruation was almost 17. In 1950 it was 13.5. By 1980 it had dropped to 11.5, with boys showing similar acceleration in their development.[2]

Between the mental stimulation from the media and the acceleration of physical maturity, our children are pressured to act on their sexuality at an age unprecedented in Western history. We adults catch the fever. We worry that our Bret must be dating by the sixth grade or he will be passed over socially forever. Children are urged to act like mini-adults instead of allowed to be children. They may look chic and sound sophisticated, but they're still just kids. Despite the sincerity of our Christian beliefs, many of us as parents have unwittingly become caught up in the world's ways by rushing our children into sex.

Me First

In today's world it is considered an unacceptable limitation of personal freedom to suggest that we find contentment and meaning outside ourselves. Consequently we give ourselves the green light to "do our own thing." We are convinced that if we thwart our self-centered desires we will irreparably damage our psyches. Although there are some dissenting voices, the majority of today's therapists reinforce this worldview by focusing heavily on what we want, need, and feel. Our children are growing up in a world where the "me generation" is alive and thriving. Unfortunately, many Christian parents have been seduced by the world and have adopted this unbiblical self-focus.

Certainly even Christians must have some self-awareness. You can't love yourself as God commands (Matthew 22:39) unless you know who you are. Therefore, some time spent in introspection is necessary. But it is equally important that you look outside yourself. You can't really love God or others as God commands (Matthew 22:36-39) unless you have a working knowledge of who others are.

Heeding the call to "look out for number one" leaves its mark on our sexuality as parents and subsequently on our children through our example. Accepting the "me first" concept can lead us to justify loosening our moral standards, having an affair, or changing partners in order to meet our needs. The fallout of these worldly compromises can be devastating to the sexual development of our children. While we Christians accept the fact that man's basic nature is selfish, we must overcome that worldly perspective in our own thinking through God's help.

The Blurring of the Sexes

When my friend Jane was growing up, she remembers being taught all about her "privates" while her brother's genitals were referred to as his "business." Another couple I know has a unique way of distinguishing between their little boy and little girl when the children display their assertive, keep-up-with-the-best-of-them attitudes. When their son exhibits his bold side they agree with the expression, "He has testicles!" But when their daughter is into her daring-do, they conclude instead, "She has ovum!"

Today, both sets of parents would probably be branded sexist for making such distinctions. Conscientious parents who dare to distinguish between male and female propensities are made to feel that they have doomed their children to stifling roles that can only lead to unhappiness and limitation of their abilities. Yielding to this clamor to raise our kids in a nonsexist manner is another way Christian parents unthinkingly buy into the world's approach to the facts of life.

Males and females are more alike than different in the grand scheme of things. We digest food the same way. We are emotional. We wonder about life. We need love and care to develop properly. We desire to be important. However, to denigrate our male/female differences because of our many similarities is a loss to us as individuals and a major and tragic loss to society. The real message of any liberation movement is to allow people the freedom to be who and what they are. Despite all the hullabaloo, who we are, more often than not, follows traditional male or female models.

After extensive research, Jo Durden-Smith and Diane De Simone, coauthors of _Sex and the Brain_, concluded what we who love the Word already know: There are subtle and significant differences in the way men and women think and approach life. A man's language skills are concentrated in the left brain, but they are divided more evenly in the woman's brain. Female hormones influence the production of "good" cholesterol, while testosterone in the man increases the low-density lipoprotein which clogs vessels, resulting in a risk of heart disease double that of the female. Males are more sensitive to light. Women are more sensitive to sound and have a better sense of smell. Estrogen strengthens the immune system, resulting in increased risk of autoimmune disorders in women but greater resistance to infection. Women have twice the body fat of men, which settles in the most appropriate places—according to our sense of aesthetics!

God made us male and female (Genesis 1:27). We each have a genetic inclination to act and think in a way that more than remotely matches our physical bodies. The vast majority of us will grow up comfortable with the bodies and orientation God gave us. Other than being as clear as possible on God's message to us as men and women, you don't need to go to great extremes ensuring the masculinity or femininity of your children. Relax—God took care of that for you!

What about children who display confusion over gender-identification? I would certainly intervene if my child were displaying some obvious problems such as habitual cross-dressing, never playing with appropriate-sex toys, or avoiding play with same-sex peers. However, I would not set out on a crusade if my boy chose to play with dolls. After all, he will probably be a daddy some day, and he needs to practice parenting as much as the little girls do. I wouldn't even panic if he chooses to play the mommy from time to time. Children normally practice role-switching as a way of learning about life. I remember with great fondness my own childhood days when being Roy Rogers seemed so much more adventuresome than playing Dale Evans.

For those who fear producing children who are too sexist, I remind you that establishing a nonsexist environment at home is a nearly impossible task. Despite our best (or worst, depending on your viewpoint) efforts, more often than not Jason will use the doll leg he has pulled off as a gun to kill an enemy, while Jennifer will nurse the poor doll back to health. There is nothing wrong with children expressing themselves in ways that fall into female or male categories or in occasionally investigating the domain of the opposite sex. Both are simply natural explorations of the grown-up world. (The issue of homosexuality is discussed more fully in Chapter 13.)

Winning the War against the World

A newspaper article recently reported that the thriving business of an enterprising group of children ranging in age from eight to 13 had been closed down. They weren't running a lemonade stand or a lawn-mowing service in this small New England town. Having been initiated into sex by adult friends and relatives, these kids developed a scheme for sharing adult clients in a kid-operated prostitution ring. The community was stunned, the newspaper stated. I was stunned, even though I've dealt with the evidence and aftermath of sexual abuse in almost every abused client I have counseled.

How does something like this happen? Children do not naturally involve themselves in sexual activities with partners of a different age and power level. They are taught. The child prostitutes learned from the adults in their lives that their young bodies were valuable commodities. And having no reference point for seeing themselves differently, these youngsters converted a humiliating, shame-based experience into an issue of power and money. In a perverse way they reframed their reality.

Abused children undoubtedly hate what is happening to them. I'm sure that they fantasize how kindly and wonderfully they will treat their own children. Statistically, however, the opposite occurs. It is highly unusual to find an abusing parent who was not abused as a child.

None of us wants to adopt negative and demeaning life patterns, but we do. The power of those who modeled life for us as children is so great that, even when we understand intellectually how we should act, our experience is the prime motivation in our behavior. The children in the small town merely modeled what they saw. How different their lives would have been had the adults around them patterned their lives after Christ.

So how do we as parents combat the influence of the world in our own kids? I have two suggestions: Model positive sexual attitudes, and give them the facts they need at the appropriate time.

Model Positive Sexual Attitudes

It is highly unlikely that your children view the physical dimension of your sexual relationship firsthand. But you model a sexual attitude nevertheless. Every interaction you have with the opposite sex says something about how you feel about that sex. How you react when a sexual topic is brought up, how you handle sexual humor, and how you express yourself physically toward the opposite sex in public are carefully noted and filed away by your perceptive children. Whether you are loving and open or closed and cold, you send out information that influences how your children will think and act.

One of the biggest mistakes we make is *telling* our kids what to do while *acting out* something different. We find it much easier to pontificate than to live the example. You may be able to fool the boss or the fellow down the street, but you can't fool the kid who lives with you. If you want to win the war against the world, you've got to clean up your act. If you don't want your children to read or watch pornography, you can't read it or watch it either. If you want them to treat members of the opposite sex with respect, you must also— especially those in your own family. If you want them to grow up valuing God's view of sex, marriage, and family, your commitment to these values must be clearly visible to them every day.

The Importance of Home and Faith

Research shows that children who postpone sex until marriage are more likely to come from happy homes in which they are able to communicate openly and have respect for their parents. Secular studies such as the Andrews Quality of Life Study indicate that people achieve a sense of well-being when they have their family and sex life in order. The more traditional the home, with parental roles clearly defined, the greater the influence on children to wait for sex. A child with a stable, orderly, affectionate, and caring home environment will be able to take the time needed to make responsible sexual decisions.[3]

Furthermore, religious and secular research consistently shows a positive relationship between religious activity and responsible sexual decision-making. For example, one study indicated that 38.8 percent of the young women who attended religious services at least once a week had sex, whereas 65.4 percent of those who attended less than once a month had sex. Of those women saying religion was very important, 45 percent had sex, while 60 percent of those who considered religion somewhat important or not important had sex.[4]

This trend is not limited to one particular religious persuasion or denomination. But just being from a family that regularly attends church isn't the answer. The underlying factor is the seriousness with which the child holds his or her religious beliefs. The child who has been helped to develop and practice a strong personal faith is better equipped to resist the world's negative influence.

When parents ask me, "What's the most effective thing we can do to help our children be sexually responsible?" the answer is easy: Keep your marriage strong and sound, and encourage personal religious faith.

What About the Single-parent Home?

Not all children grow up in traditional two-parent families. Two out of five children in the United States will spend at least part of their growing up years in a single-parent home. What is the effect of the single-parent household on a child's moral responsibility?

Research tells us that children from single-parent homes are more permissive sexually, particularly if the home is headed by a female. Despite trends in joint custody, nine out of ten children living with one parent live with the mother.[5] The more the living arrangements diverge from a traditional family, the greater the permissiveness.

Clearly, the modeling effects of the single parent's dating behavior are at work. Sad to say, I have heard many parents try to rationalize the effects of their behavior on their children because their own needs were so great. I certainly sympathize with anyone reeling from divorce. However, the emotional impact of different men or women parading through a child's home can be far-reaching, especially if the parent is sexually active.

In view of all the pressures we face in the secular world, how can we be the effective examples our children need? We also need an example. God instructs us to know His nature through the study of His Word and His living model, Jesus. He also enables us to break out of old, unhealthy patterns and establish new, productive ones. When we live the life Christ wants us to live, we don't have to fear the example we are setting for our children. We will be models that will influence their lives positively whatever their circumstances.

Give Them the Facts

As important as your example is, your kids need more. Even when you are succeeding as a positive model of sexuality for your children, they can't get all the information from you they need about sex by osmosis. They need "the facts of life," and you must communicate the facts to them. Your children are more likely to develop a conservative sexual outlook if you are the primary source of their sexual information.

As well-meaning parents, most of us set out with an agenda we intend to follow to ensure that our children get the factual information about sex they need. There are two problems with this agenda, however. First, we are usually five years off in our estimate of the age of perceived need for sexual information. Second, we frequently never quite get around to having the "big talk" about sex, let alone recurrent little ones.

Just how little timely, factual material about sex parents share with their children may surprise you. In one long-term study, 35 percent of seventh-grade girls had begun their periods, but 20 percent of them had never been told anything about menstruation.[6] Furthermore, 50 percent of the girls had never discussed the father's role in sexuality, and 68 percent had been told nothing about birth control.

In a study by Koblinsky and Atkinson with young children, 75 percent of the children's mothers and 50 percent of their fathers had discussions with them about pregnancy. But only 15 percent of the mothers and 8 percent of the fathers mentioned intercourse.[7]

In one survey of college students, most had little recollection of much being discussed in their families about sex. The strongest messages they reportedly received were that sex has a "dangerous" quality about it and "pregnancy can lead to terrible things."[8]

The tragedy of the erratic, hit-or-miss parental method of dispensing the facts is that misconceptions about sex can flourish for years. I remember as a child being terrified to be in an elevator with men because I thought their sperm was just floating around them and I would surely get pregnant. I also remember worrying that I would somehow inadvertently lose my virginity, even though I wasn't sure what made me a virgin in the first place. Teens have enough to worry about figuring out who they are without carrying the additional burden of misinformation.

The greater the number and range of sexual topics discussed by a child's parents, the less likely that child will initiate intercourse.[9] This fact directly assaults the argument that sharing information about sex contributes to sexual permissiveness. There are no studies that show this claim to be true. In the many reports on the results of access to contraceptive information, no relationship exists between knowledge and increased use. There is plenty of evidence to the contrary, however. Lack of birth control information is not a deterrent for the teen who chooses to be sexually active.

How Strong *Is* Peer Pressure?

I frequently hear parents absolving themselves of their responsibility to teach anything to their teenagers on the grounds that peers are the only ones with any influence. I would agree with that line of thinking if you do not establish an early pattern of directing your child's learning and being askable. For those who establish such patterns, your influence does not stop at the magical age of 13, although it's greater during your child's early teen years.

One study in 1977 clearly demonstrated that a child's mother is his or her primary sexual authority and influence, with sex education classes and materials second, and the media third.[10] There are no studies specifying that information from one parent or the other is superior. What does matter is that information is given. The fact is, the mom is the one who most frequently fills that role. Care needs to be taken by the single and/or working mother not to relinquish her important role unless she sees to it that the father or another qualified person can share the responsibility with her.

When sex information comes from peers there is greater sexual involvement. Both boys and girls are influenced to be permissive by peer approval of permissiveness. However, strong peer pressure affects a boy most if that pressure is in the direction of being sexually active. Girls are more likely to be influenced if the pressure is in the direction of abstinence.[11]

With parents communicating so little sex information directly, allowing so many mixed and confusing messages to flourish, is it any wonder that teens today are not making sound decisions? Is it fair that we ask our children to understand our hit-or-miss approach? Inadequate information results in guilt feelings and needless anxieties that contribute greatly to the high level of stress so characteristic of our society. Correct information from you about sex is your child's birthright. Part Two of this book was written expressly to help you provide your children with the timely, accurate information they need.

Our society has done a superlative job of convincing us parents that we are inept, inconsequential, and more damaging than helpful in the lives of our children. We are reminded that we're at fault if our kids turn out bad, while our kids are stroked for having "survived" us. The plethora of parenting "experts" with their diversity of opinions only makes matters worse. It's difficult to raise and train children in today's world.

The soundest and least contradictory parenting book I've found is also the oldest. Consider the wisdom of these passages as they apply to your role as primary example and information-giver in your child's sex education:

- Fathers, do not exasperate your children; instead bring them up in the training and instruction of the Lord (Ephesians 6:4).
- Impress [God's commandments] on your children. Talk about them when you sit at home and when you walk along the road, when you lie down and when you get up (Deuteronomy 6:6,7).
- Train a child in the way he should go, and when he is old he will not turn from it (Proverbs 22:6).
- Do not withhold discipline from a child (Proverbs 23:13).
- Children, obey your parents in the Lord, for this is right (Ephesians 6:1).

- Honor your father and your mother (Exodus 20:12).
- A wise son brings joy to his father (Proverbs 10:1).
- Whoever loves discipline loves knowledge, but he who hates correction is stupid (Proverbs 12:1).

We need not apologize for being in charge. We are to be models of sexual purity for our children. We are to train them, instruct them, and discipline them. As parents we are to be in the world but not of it, so our children can grow up the same way.

3

Sex Is Not a Sin

In the 1800s a pioneer judicial reformer from Louisiana, Edward Livingston, took it upon himself to pen a model law code. He deliberately left out a number of sexual crimes because, "as every crime must be defined, the details of such a definition would inflict a lasting wound on the morals of the people."[1] In Livingston's mind, depravity would be encouraged if such details were disclosed, even for the sake of justice.

Historically, facing issues of sexuality openly and honestly has not been one of America's strengths. We laugh at the Victorians of the 1800s who covered their piano "limbs" so as not to offend. But many of us remember with chagrin the days when uttering the word "pregnant" in public was a moral outrage. A woman was "with child" or "expecting."

Yes, we've come a long way in the last few years, but our treatment of sexuality has yet to become natural. Our discussions tend to be riddled with jokes and innuendos, reflective of our continued discomfort. Or we opt for the sterile medical approach, hoping that tongue-twisting terminology and white lab coats will immunize us against this filthy disease.

We have inherited the mind-set in America that sex is dirty. Sex is not only a sin, we think, but it's the *worst* sin, perhaps even an unforgivable sin. The body is evil, its functions are despicable, and physical pleasure is of the devil. The only way to glorify God in this sex-crazed, sinful world is to be separated, set-apart, celibate sourpusses.

Sound familiar? Straight from old Granny Gert, you say? I suggest that you take a closer look at yourself to make sure some of these negative concepts aren't tainting your own attitudes about sex. Being good sex educators for our children requires that we grasp the God-ordained purpose of sex as a unifier, a pleasure bond, and the means of procreation. Sex is not a sin; it's a gift from God to be experienced within the marriage relationship. The body is not evil; it's the dwelling place of the Holy Spirit. Satan is not the author of physical pleasure; God designed us to enjoy sex within the guidelines of His Word. It is through our faith that we help our children make sense of life, including sexuality. Sex is important, good, sacred, and honorable. The Bible tells us so.

What Does the Bible Say?

Both Old and New Testament present a positive sexual image. Genesis states that God deliberately created male and female (1:27), that they were naked and unashamed (2:25), and that it was very good (1:31). Woman was given to man to be "a helper suitable for him" (2:18). She was to be a complement to him, a "complete-ment," one of two pieces that make a finished puzzle. God designed the mutual propensity of men and women to desire soul mates. We are to realize that fulfillment and contentment within the married state.

Mosaic law also acknowledged the sanctity of sex within marriage. Exodus 21:10 reminds men to give their wives their "marital rights." The admonitions in Exodus 19:15 and 1 Samuel 21:4 to temporarily abstain from sex are related to preparation for worship. Abstinence was also commanded before and after menstruation and childbirth for obvious hygienic reasons, but it was also only a temporary abstinence.

Deuteronomy 24:5 tells us much about the importance of marriage and sex to the early Hebrew: "If a man has recently married, he must not be sent to war or have any other duty laid on him. For one year he is to be free to stay at home and bring happiness to the wife he has married." I've often wondered how such a plan would work today!

A close look at the New Testament reveals the same positive approach to sex and marriage. Jesus reminds us in Matthew 19:4-6 that God's purpose in creating us male and female was for us to marry and become one flesh. More than a nodding approval of wedding festivities and marriage is suggested by Jesus' first miracle, converting water to wine at the marriage feast in Cana (John 2:1-11). And two of His parables have wedding feasts as their backdrop (Matthew 22:1-14; 25:1-13).

The Scriptural metaphor of Christ as the bridegroom and the church as His bride (John 3:27-29; Revelation 19:7-9; 21:2,9) would be senseless if God considered sex sinful, harmful, and unclean. Paul also linked the relationship of husband and wife with the relationship of Christ and His church. The apostle encourages men to strengthen the marriage bond by loving their wives as Christ loves the church (Ephesians 5:25). Women are instructed to submit to their husbands as to the Lord (Ephesians 5:22).

Paul also wrote about the importance of the sexual dimension in marriage:

> The husband should fulfill his marital duty to his wife, and likewise the wife to her husband. The wife's body does not belong to her alone but also to her husband. In the same way, the husband's body does not belong to him alone but also to his wife. Do not deprive each other except by mutual consent and for a time, so that you may devote yourselves to prayer. Then come together again so that Satan will not tempt you because of your lack of self-control (1 Corinthians 7:3-5).

In 1 Timothy 4:4,5 Paul gives further insight into the New Testament position on love, sex, and marriage. Speaking against false teachers who told Christians that marriage was wrong, Paul wrote: "For everything God created is good, and nothing is to be rejected if it is received with thanksgiving, because it is consecrated by the word of God and prayer."

What Went Wrong?

Clearly, the perception of sex as dirty and sinful didn't derive from the Bible. Something happened between the first century and today which caused Christians and society in general to regard sex and sexuality as impure instead of pure, ugly instead of beautiful. We can trace this decline historically through the periods of the early church, the church fathers, the Middle Ages, the Reformation, and the movements of Puritanism and Pietism.

The Early Church

Four major influences impacted the sexual thinking of the first-century church: Greek culture, the popularity of asceticism, persecution, and the expectation of an immediate Second Coming.

Even though Rome ruled the world politically, Greek thought, art, and language exerted a powerful cultural influence. The Greeks theorized that man's nature was dualistic, comprised of two separate entities: body and soul. To them the body was insignificant; you could overindulge your physical appetites without affecting your soul. Dualists saw nothing wrong with sexual immorality, so it was rampant in the culture which surrounded the early church.

The licentiousness of the pagan world was repugnant to Christians, so they rightly distanced themselves from it by adopting a lifestyle that disavowed any association with sexual excesses. But in the process of separating themselves from sexual immorality, some Christians mistakenly identified sex and sexuality, instead of immorality, as the source of the problem. If God is against evil, they thought, He must also be against the body that performs it. Many Christians concluded that all physical pleasures, including sex within marriage, were to be avoided if Christlikeness was to be achieved. Thus Christian asceticism was born, a philosophy that eventually produced the monastic system and vows of celibacy in the service of God. This fruitless diversion could have been avoided if Christians had taken seriously Paul's warning against such prohibitions in Colossians 2:20-23.

Many believers opted for celibacy for other reasons. Persecution was common in the early church. Facing the prospect of hardship and possibly martyrdom, many believers held little hope of reaching old age. Not wanting to leave behind a family in need of care, they chose not to marry and/or bear children. This is the context in which Paul wrote, "It is good for a man not to marry" (1 Corinthians 7:1).

Furthermore, the early Christians believed that Christ's Second Coming was imminent, so many of them rejected worldly and physical pleasures. Why marry, have children, and work toward long-term family goals if there was going to be no long term?

All these influences in the first century combined to establish attitudes and practices toward sex which were far from biblical.

The Church Fathers

Things got worse over the next few hundred years. Origen, the well-respected theologian, believed that Adam and Eve didn't have intercourse until after the Fall. He felt that God's intention for reproduction centered instead around some mysterious or angelic process that eliminated the sin element. To Origen, intercourse was double jeopardy: committing original sin and having sex with a daughter of Satan (that is, any female). Origen was committed to this view to the point of castrating himself on the basis of Matthew 19:12 in order to better serve the kingdom of God. He was one of the first church leaders to suggest the concept of the monastery.

Jerome, one of the greatest church fathers, suggested that touching a woman was evil and that marriage made praying difficult. In his thinking, married saints only managed to remain saints if they didn't have sex after marriage!

By A.D. 300, being a Christian was no longer dangerous politically. But according to Augustine, a believer's sexual desires still kept him in a perilous position. He declared that sexual intercourse, even with one's spouse, was bad; celibacy and self-denial were good and the pathway to God. Pope Gregory (590-604) reinforced Augustine's conclusions by declaring marital intercourse sinful.

The Middle Ages

During the Middle Ages, eliminating sin was equated with avoiding sexual intercourse, sexual thoughts, and women. All women were viewed as sensual, seductive, corrupt temptresses who were beyond understanding. As a result of this influence, even Christian women, who had been active in the ministry from Jesus' time, were no longer allowed influence in the church hierarchy.

Despite all the negatives surrounding sex, only priests, nuns, and monks took vows of chastity. Common folk did whatever they pleased, and the nobility appeared to be pious while elevating infidelity to a fine art.

Thomas Aquinas is noted for attempting to unify the many factions of Christianity during the 1200s. Influenced greatly by Aristotle, Aquinas believed that man lived and communicated with God through reason. Sex was a distraction to godliness because it interfered with the contemplative life.

Aquinas viewed women as inferior to men, but not wholly evil. He felt that sex was basically sinful, and that women were often used by Satan to seduce men away from God. But he conceded that marital intercourse was allowed by God for procreation and to keep men from worse sins.

The Reformation

With the coming of Martin Luther (1483-1546) and the Reformation, a turnaround began. Luther first sought God through the ascetic life of a monk. But when he grasped the significance of salvation by grace, he devoted his life to restoring biblical concepts in the church on many issues, including sexuality.

The sex drive, Luther declared, was as natural and necessary as the drive to eat and drink. God's grace sanctifies sex, and faith transforms marriage from a purely physical relationship into an expression of Christian love. No longer was man's sexuality to be denied or his body and soul viewed as separate. Sexuality was to be expressed as God intended.

John Calvin developed Luther's concepts even further. He called for an end to celibacy for those living the religious life, although he encouraged a rather strict inner asceticism designed to produce a moral lifestyle.

Puritanism and Pietism

Calvin directly influenced the spread of Puritanism in England and the American colonies. Since God alone determined who was to be saved, the individual Puritan pursued morality, good works, and stringent self-discipline as an indication that he had been chosen. Moderation was the byword, especially in matters of personal pleasure such as sex. Puritanism deteriorated into legalism, equating sexual restraint, even in marriage, with godliness.

Pietism also influenced American thought. The focus of Pietism on inward holiness required the exclusion of all worldly pleasures. Sex was pleasurable and therefore shunned.

In the centuries since the New Testament was written, church leaders and theologians have provided a positive influence in numerous aspects of Christian living. But many of their contributions to the church in the area of sexuality were determined more by ignorance and reaction to the attitudes of the day than by sound biblical scholarship. Overall we may conclude that little good has been said about sex since New Testament times. As a result, the believer's sex life has been separated from his spiritual life. It's time that they are integrated again as God intended. We owe it to our children to help them learn to be biblically sexual.

A 3000-Year-Old Marriage Manual

Since the church historically has struggled with sex education, it's no wonder that Song of Songs in the Old Testament, written by Solomon about 1000 B.C., has absolutely mystified many church leaders. Why is a collection of love poems included among the prophetic revelations of God? There must be a higher interpretation than just the love, marriage, and sex relationship of a king and his bride.

For many years the Jews theorized that the Song was an allegory describing the love between Jehovah and Israel. Origen and other church fathers wondered if it didn't in some mystical way elaborate on the relationship of the individual soul to God or Christ. Many Christians even today relate it to the love of Christ for the church.

A literal interpretation, although first suggested as early as A.D. 429, has had general acceptance only in contemporary times. But there is every reason to believe that since the Lord holds marriage and sex in high esteem He would include His guidelines for this relationship in Scripture. Nowhere in the Bible do we find a more graphic, detailed description of the romantic, sexual side of marriage than in Song of Songs.

Song of Songs (also called Song of Solomon) tells the story of King Solomon and his special bride, identified only as a Shulammite girl from the countryside. The story includes reminiscences of their courtship, wedding, and wedding night. They resolve typical marital problems and in general give us a delightful glimpse of what married life designed by God is meant to be. For a helpful, detailed explanation of the symbolism and message of the Song, I recommend Joseph Dillow's book, *Solomon on Sex* (Thomas Nelson).

The Glories of Married Love

In the first part of the book (Song of Songs 1:1–5:1), the bride recalls the early days of their courtship, their wedding, and the wedding banquet. These chapters stress the importance of saving physical love for marriage and basing marriage on a sound friendship. Also, helpful guidelines for married love are revealed, such as improving sexual response by thinking positively about your partner and building your anticipation of being together.

Finally, the couple finds the royal bedroom to be a sanctuary conducive to relaxation and romance. No expense is spared to make this room a delight for the lovers. Long and leisurely conversations take place there, particularly after lovemaking. How does your bedroom compare?

The Shulammite girl is apparently worth coming home to, for she takes pride in her personal appearance. Her efforts are not in vain, for the king verbalizes his appreciation for her. These biblical lovers never cease striving to be complimentary. I wonder why so many of us think our marriages will flourish without nourishing them in this way.

Problems in Paradise

Being married to a king didn't shelter the Shulammite girl from problems. Song of Songs 5:2–8:4 deals with sexual and other difficulties they experienced and reveals the couple's problem-solving techniques.

For example, Solomon liked late-night sex, but his bride liked her sleep. The king felt rejected, but he didn't pout or retaliate. He continued to express unconditional love and caring. He understood the principle that if you want to be loved, you must also be loving. His persistent love won his bride's heart, allowing her to change her attitude and go to him with real desire. The dance of Mahanaim (6:13–8:4) describes her erotic appeal. For any of you into bellydancing for your husband without inhibitions, you're in good company with King Solomon's bride!

Another problem they faced that many of us can relate to is a lack of time together. But they didn't leave their private time to chance; they _made_ time for each other. Good marriages require quality time together. By scheduling time alone together you let your partner know how important he or she is to you.

The couple employed four excellent problem-solving techniques to deal with their conflicts. First, each remained sensitive to the other's needs. Second, each accepted responsibility to change his or her actions. Third, each realized that changing attitudes requires a conscious effort. And fourth, each was willing to work to effect a solution. If you learn nothing else from Song of Songs, adopting these guidelines will make a world of difference in your marriage relationship.

Come Away with Me

Solomon obviously didn't believe, as many modern fellows do, that displays of affection and romance are important for courtship but not for marriage. Solomon is undeniably busy, but he keeps romance in his marriage. He still takes his bride on dates. He sometimes romances her in unexpected and impractical ways. And he strives to be creative. The Song concludes (8:5-14) with the couple vacationing in the country and reaffirming their love. The scene opens with an embrace and closes with physical love freely given in the countryside the Shulammite girl loves so much.

Questions about Sex and the Bible

Whenever I teach or counsel on what the Bible says about sex, questions invariably arise. Some of the questions are about topics which were considered hush-hush a generation ago. Other questions focus on issues which are not clearly discussed in the Bible. I want to close this chapter by responding to some of the typical questions I am asked. Maybe you're wondering about them too.

My sexual appetite isn't always as great as that of Solomon or the Shulammite girl. Do I ever have the right to turn down sex with my spouse?

Ephesians 5:21 tells us, "Submit to one another out of reverence for Christ." First Corinthians 7:3 states, "The husband should fulfill his marital duty to his wife, and likewise the wife to her husband." Regardless of your individual appetite, you are to be willingly available to your spouse except when you mutually agree to forego sex for a short time or for prayer. Headaches, tiredness, and Monday night football are *not* good excuses to say, "Not tonight, Dear."

Does that mean one spouse has the right to force sex on the other?

Absolutely not. God never wants us to violate our partner's will to fulfill our own. First Corinthians 13:5 explains that love "is not rude, it is not self-seeking." Forcing sex also violates Philippians 2:2,4: "Make my joy complete by being like-minded, having the same love, being one in spirit and purpose....Each of you should look not only to your own interests, but also to the interests of others."

Am I then free to decline lovemaking techniques my spouse wants to try because I am uncomfortable with them?

In Song of Songs the two lovers delight in each other and seemingly have few lovemaking inhibitions. Holding back or refusing to try suggestions from your spouse appears to conflict with 1 Corinthians 7:3,4. However, in areas where you feel you are being asked for more than you can give, understanding from your spouse is mandated by 1 Corinthians 13:5.

What about oral sex? Is it biblical?

Oral sex is not mentioned specifically in the Bible, but many feel it is condoned in the Bible's general approval of sexual activity between husband and wife. Some believe that Song of Songs 2:3 refers to oral sex since "fruit" was sometimes used in the Bible as a euphemism for male genitals. As Solomon's love poem suggests, what is acceptable in lovemaking is only limited by what is comfortable and enriching to each partner.

What about masturbation?

Like oral sex, masturbation isn't mentioned by name in the Bible. Some think that Onan was masturbating when he "spilled his semen on the ground" (Genesis 38:8-10), for which God punished him with death. But the act described here is *coitus interruptus* or withdrawal. Onan was punished for disobeying God's command to perpetuate the family line. The only other biblical references to what may be masturbation are Leviticus 22:4 and 2 Samuel 3:29 in the Revised Standard Version. But these verses are also inconclusive.

Thomas Aquinas considered masturbation an unnatural,

mortal sin, worse than adultery, rape, incest, or prostitution. Penances for masturbation ranged from one to three years, depending on whether the offender was a cleric.

As the church lost its influence after the Renaissance, arguments against masturbation focusing on the threat to health carried greater weight. Tissot, an eighteenth-century Swiss physician and adviser to the Vatican, declared that masturbation caused excessive blood flow to the brain, resulting in insanity and impotence. This inaccurate link between masturbation and insanity remained strong until the 1950s.

Eighteenth-century philosopher Immanuel Kant feared that masturbation among the youth would ruin society because the future generation would be unable to have children, become prematurely old, and be intellectually weak. And the first book of psychiatry in the United States, published during the 1800s, identified the symptoms of masturbation as weakness, dimness of sight, epilepsy, and loss of memory. Somewhere along the way, "hair on the palms" was thrown in for extra measure.

Today there is still a strong diversity of opinion about masturbation among Christians. Some feel that since so few participants have peace about it we have a right to be concerned. But considering our historically inaccurate and disturbing input on the subject, how could anyone feel otherwise? We will discuss masturbation further in Chapter 13.

Are sexual sins worse than other sins?

Jesus had no more difficulty forgiving sexual sins than any other kind. Mary Magdalene was a prostitute, and Jesus completely forgave her, as He did the adulteress in John 8 and the woman at the well in John 4. Indeed, Jesus was more tolerant of sexual sins than the legalism and hypocrisy of the Pharisees and Scribes, declaring in Matthew 21:31 that tax collectors and prostitutes would get into heaven before they would!

Following Jesus' example, we are to condemn sexual sin but not judge the sexual sinner. And we who have not sinned sexually are to avoid a holier-than-thou attitude toward repentant sexual sinners, because they are forgiven just as we are.

However, Paul specifically cautioned us against sexual sins, pointing out a significant difference between them and all other sins:

> He who unites himself with the Lord is one with him in spirit. Flee from sexual immorality. All other sins a man commits are outside his body, but he who sins sexually sins against his own body. Do you not know that your body is a temple of the Holy Spirit, who is in you, whom you have received from God? (1 Corinthians 6:17-19).

How can I please God as a parent in my sexual life?

First Thessalonians 4:3-7 provides an excellent answer. Paul begins, "It is God's will that you should be sanctified: that you should avoid sexual immorality" (verse 3). Paul doesn't say we are to avoid sex, but sexual immorality.

Sexual purity for the single parent involves refraining from sexual intercourse. For any who try to be literal at this point by saying, "I can do anything sexually as long as I don't have intercourse," the Lord says that the law is broken when the spirit of the law is broken.

For married parents, sexual purity means remaining faithful to your partner. Again, the spirit of the law can be broken if you are physically faithful but commit mental or emotional adultery. Furthermore, the Bible implies that what you as husband and wife mutually agree upon for your sexual lives has God's blessing.

Paul continues, "Each of you should learn to control his own body in a way that is holy and honorable, not in passionate lust like the heathen, who do not know God" (verses 4 and 5). I regard this statement as our biblical mandate for sex education. You are not to guess about how your body works; you are to learn about it in order to master it and avoid lust. Lust is a personal, intense sexual desire or craving. Sexuality which is not based on God's standard or grounded in Scripture is diminished to nothing more than self-gratification.

Mastery over lust only comes as you understand and accept the sexual person you are.

Verses 6 and 7 state: "In this matter no one should wrong his brother or take advantage of him.... For God did not call us to be impure, but to live a holy life." For our purposes, perhaps we should paraphrase the first sentence, "In sexual matters, no one should wrong his husband, wife, son, or daughter." Rape, pedophilia, sexual molestation, incest, deceiving or manipulating another to obtain sexual gratification—tragically, all these despicable forms of sexual abuse are happening in families across our country. God's plan for us as parents is that we never take advantage of our spouse or children sexually. Rather, our relationship with them is to be marked by purity and holy living.

4

For Mom (and the Man in Her Life)

At 11 years old, Alyson and Annette were still formulating their concept of marriage when they heard Pastor Bob give a talk on the subject. The girls were all ears until he started talking about marriages made in heaven. As the pastor continued on with his talk, Alyson couldn't let go of that perplexing thought. Her dreamy, schoolgirl fantasy of marriage was being seriously challenged.

Finally she turned to Annette, whose mind was stuck at the same roadblock. "I don't want a marriage made in heaven," Alyson announced to her friend a little too loudly. "Being married to God doesn't sound very romantic!" Annette nodded her agreement.

Well, Alyson and Annette, sometimes being married to a down-to-earth, flesh-and-blood husband isn't very romantic either. And countless numbers of husbands have admitted to me that the women they married aren't always the steamy sex goddesses they hoped for. I believe in marriages made in heaven, but I also believe it takes a lot of work, love, and prayer to enjoy heaven on earth in a marriage relationship.

Mom and Dad, if you want to be a good example of biblical

sexuality for your children, and communicate effectively to them what they need to know about sex, your sexual relationship must be alive, well, and growing. You need to understand your sexual organs and how they work. You need to understand your sexual arousal system and what turns it on and off. You need to be in touch with your own sexual needs and desires. And you need to understand your partner's sexuality and needs as well as your own in order to maintain a positive, mutually-rewarding sexual relationship.

This chapter highlights the woman's sexual system, and the next chapter focuses on the man's sexual system. Whether you are a mom or a dad, I urge you to read both chapters and talk about them with your partner.

Becoming the World's Authority on You

A patient came in to be examined by my husband, who is a gynecologist-obstetrician. "I have cancer, Dr. Mayo," she announced with alarm. "I just had to see you today."

"All right, Mrs. Jones, show me the cancer," Joe said after examining her. "I don't see anything abnormal."

"There, Doctor, that little lump."

"That's not cancer, Mrs. Jones. That's your clitoris!"

It's all-too-common incidents like these that make me realize how ignorant some women are about their sexual organs. It is a rare woman who has done much exploring of her own body. Everything is hidden, and nice girls don't touch down there anyway, right? Let's take time to make sure we are clear on body parts and functions.

Your Largest Sex Organ

The largest and most sensitive sex organ in your body is your skin. Remember how excited you were when you first held hands or kissed someone you cared for? Just brushing him on the shoulder as you passed in the hall at school made you a basket case for your next class. We never lose the need for this type of touching, even when we have access to far more intimate touching behavior. Many married women report greater arousal from kissing and touching than they ever experience from intercourse.

Breasts have been so eroticized by our society that the woman who is not especially responsive to having them touched may think she is abnormal. No matter what society or your husband says, you must accept your individualized responses and understand that, when it comes to sex, you are the world's foremost expert on you.

By the way, for some women, breast-feeding an infant can be arousing enough to cause orgasm. This is not abnormal or perverted but a normal body response and one to which no guilt should be attached or deeper meaning attributed.

The External Organs

The fat pad that covers the female genitals is called the *mons*. The *pubic hair* located there serves as protection from irritation and perspiration. The folds that cover a woman's vaginal and urethral openings are the *labia* (majora and minora, big and little), but are often referred to as *lips* to the vaginal orifice. The color and shape of these two sets of lips are as unique to you as the shape of your nose. All the external parts together are referred to as the *vulva*.

Near the top of the labia is the *clitoral shaft*. This shaft ends in the *clitoral hood* which protects the delicate *clitoris*. At the height of sexual excitement the clitoris retracts under the hood. Some have wrongly concluded that greater excitement would result if the clitoris were exposed by removing the hood. Several years ago such procedures were advocated in a number of popular women's magazines. But the only thing you will get if you cut or remove the hood is greater pain! Today such procedures are regulated in most states by the medical community.

The clitoris compares most closely to the glans of the penis. Both are rich in nerves, highly sensitive, and responsive. Since men associate touching their penises with pleasure, they often mistakenly conclude that a woman would like her clitoris stroked. Many women find this painful, preferring indirect stimulation through the caressing of the surrounding skin areas.

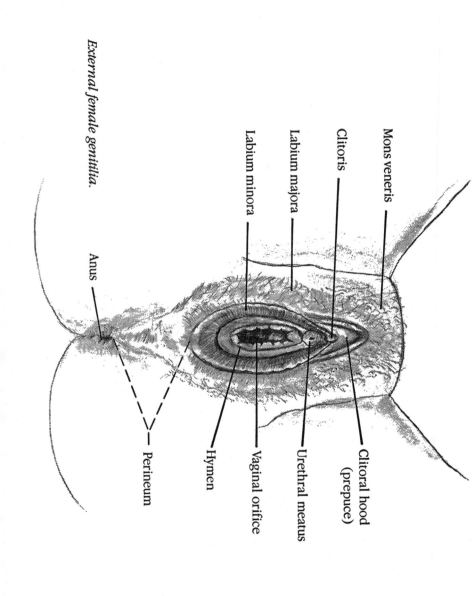

External female genitilia.

Mons veneris

Clitoris

Labium majora

Labium minora

Anus

Perineum

Hymen

Vaginal orifice

Urethral meatus

Clitoral hood
(prepuce)

Above the larger vaginal opening is the small urethral opening. Unlike the male urethra which conducts urine *and* sperm, the female urethra has no reproductive function.

The appearance of the vaginal opening, which in no way is a gaping hole, is somewhat dependent on the *hymen* or its remnants. The hymen is a delicate membrane that rarely covers the vaginal opening completely. It has no known physiological use and is found only in humans.

You are probably aware of the great psychological significance of the hymen. For ages an unbroken hymen has been regarded as the mark of virginity. But a very flexible hymen can withstand intercourse and a more delicate one can be torn accidentally without intercourse. So the condition of the hymen is not a reliable test to determine who has and has not had intercourse.

Between the bottom of the vaginal opening and the anus is an area known as the *perineum*. After childbirth, stitches may be needed here. All the external organs are held in place by powerful muscles that in themselves have a great deal to do with sexual responsiveness.

The Internal Organs

The *vagina* is a collapsed tube capable of great expansion. (Don't forget to warn your daughters about the line a few scheming young men have used: "Let's see if we fit." It has no scientific validity until penises grow as large as babies' heads!) There are few nerve endings in the three to four inches of the vagina's main body, but the section closest to the opening is extremely sensitive and responsive. The *Bartholin glands*, located in the same area, are of very little use functionally, since vaginal lubrication occurs directly through the walls.

The *uterus* is suspended in the abdomen by ligaments. During pregnancy it houses the growing child, nourishing it through the rich network of blood vessels in its inner layer. When a woman is not pregnant, this inner layer is sloughed off about once every month. This is called *menstruation* or,

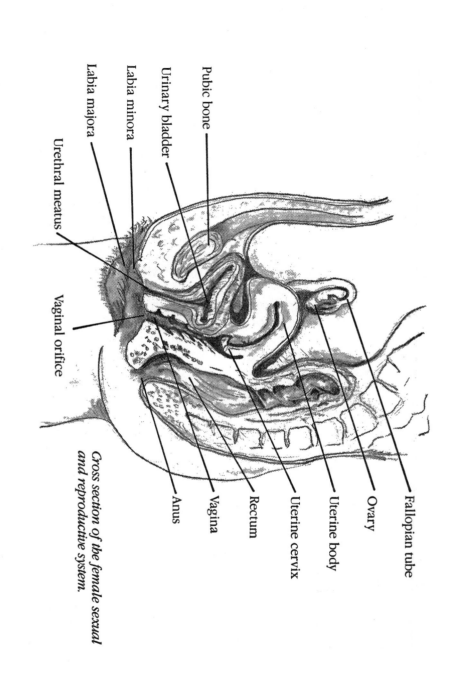

Pubic bone

Urinary bladder

Labia minora

Labia majora

Urethral meatus

Vaginal orifice

Anus

Vagina

Rectum

Uterine cervix

Uterine body

Ovary

Fallopian tube

Cross section of the female sexual and reproductive system.

more commonly, your period. Like the vagina, the uterus has few nerve endings (all mothers sigh in relief!), but the powerful muscles that surround its pear shape are capable of expelling a child at birth.

Ovaries are small, almond-shaped structures that have a dual function: producing ova (eggs) and manufacturing female hormones (estrogen and progesterone). At birth the ovaries contain thousands of immature eggs. After first menstruation, these eggs randomly mature within follicles and burst through the ovary walls at the rate of approximately one per month.

Attached directly to the uterus, but not to the ovaries, are the bilateral *Fallopian tubes*. These cilia-lined tubes are the site of fertilization. The contractions of their walls and cilia usher the developing ovum into the uterus where implantation occurs. Cutting and tying the tubes is a common means of sterilization.

A Woman's Sexual Response

When a woman is effectively stimulated, she focuses on the sexual activity while becoming progressively oblivious to other stimuli. We can generalize about some responses, but remember that each woman's exact responses are unique to her. Sexual excitement may progress rapidly or develop unevenly. Muscles tighten, circulation increases, skin is flushed, and breathing becomes heavy. Other physical responses may include toes curling, drooling, contorted faces, and funny noises. From this description we may wonder why any of us pursue activity that causes us to behave in such a crazy fashion!

Orgasm is the pleasurable though subjectively defined goal of sexual intercourse for most couples. For women, the most intense sensations occur in the lower third of the vagina as blood flows into the area and the surrounding muscles contract. Although most women focus heavily on the stimulation of the clitoris for orgasm, there is evidence in some women of a highly responsive area on the front wall of the vagina, about two inches from the entrance, called the Grafenberg spot or

G spot. Some females find this to be secondary to the clitoris as a source of pleasure. Others depend on stimulation of the G spot by the penis as their sole source of orgasm. Still others are completely oblivious to it.

About 10 percent of the female population have physical and/or psychological problems that make it all but impossible for them to experience orgasmic pleasure. That means orgasm is within the realm of reality for the vast majority of women. Generally our sexual responsiveness slows down as we age. Men require more direct stimulation; females more attention to lubrication. It's a normal part of the aging process.

Guidelines for Good Sex

There is much more to a good sexual relationship between husband and wife than physical stimulation and orgasm. Good sex is as mental and emotional as it is physical; it's a total-person package. The following guidelines for good sex—which I call the three R's, the three C's, and the ARA formula—are aimed at your total sexual relationship. In this chapter these guidelines focus on the woman. In the next chapter we'll focus the same guidelines on the man.

The Three R's

Responsiveness. Unlike men, women can be passive sex partners. But like men, if we choose to respond, we cannot simply will it to happen. Responsiveness occurs when the parasympathetic nervous system registers the physical, mental, and emotional input it receives and causes the bodily changes typical of sexual arousal.

However, stimulation, arousal, and response can be blocked by stress and its manifestations. If you're uptight, tired, distracted, or hyper, you can't have good sex. To be sexually responsive you need to consciously remove anything that is blocking stimulation.

Relaxation. Good physical health is vital to reducing stress and thereby improving sexual responsiveness. Regular exercise not only tones the muscles but releases chemicals which produce a sense of well-being and reduce stress.

Proper diet is equally important. For several years I was stressed out daily, complete with abdominal spasms, runny nose, and emotions that plummeted into the pits. I wasn't the most sexually responsive wife in those days, but I didn't know why. Then I discovered that I was hypoglycemic and allergic to milk products. Correcting my diet relaxed me physically, emotionally, and sexually. A balanced diet is important to a balanced attitude.

Our hectic pace of life also affects our sexual responsiveness by leaving us physically and emotionally drained. Learning to relax by setting priorities and pacing ourselves cannot be overemphasized. I have found it impossible to maintain order and peace in my day without the constant presence of God gained through a morning quiet time. When I'm out of whack physically, emotionally, and spiritually, I'm also out of whack sexually.

Respect. Last week you experienced a particularly passionate and warm lovemaking session with your husband and all was right with the world. But last night your romantic Prince Charming became a fumbling gorilla in bed who could do nothing right. It was the same two bodies, the same sensitive nerve endings, and more than likely the same setting, and yet the outcome was completely different. What went wrong?

Chances are your attitude had a lot to do with it. Last week you went to bed with a fellow who brought you flowers or defended your cooking to his mother earlier in the day. Your respect for him was immense and your lovemaking heavenly. But yesterday, gorilla man forgot your birthday or left you in the kitchen after Bible study with 32 coffee cups to put away while he went to bed. He made love to you the same way, but you were about as warm and responsive as a dead fish.

If you have a hard time feeling good about the man you are married to because of what he does with his life or the way he treats you, you may very well have a hard time sexually. That's why Ephesians 5:33 instructs: "The wife must respect her husband." The Great Designer knew that a woman's relationship-oriented perspective requires more than a body for meaningful sex. Your attitude toward your husband can either enhance or destroy your sexual responsiveness to him.

And if your husband doesn't feel respected, his sexuality is affected too. He may continue to function. In fact, his appetite may double—not for sexual satisfaction but for the assurance that he is honored and desired. If you aren't impressed, his next step may be to test out his potency on someone else.

Few of us women married men we didn't respect, but we don't always feel respectful. Sometimes it's necessary to remind ourselves of the traits in our husbands we once thought we couldn't live without. Affirm him verbally and often for the traits you admire. Your attitude of respect will return, and your sexual responsiveness will rekindle.

The Three C's

Communication. A good relationship, sexual or otherwise, begins with good communication. In all my years of sexual counseling, only two couples had a lack of sexual knowledge as their sole problem. All others had a combination of concerns, with communication the most serious. The majority of sexual problems (and we all have sexual problems at some time in our lives) are eliminated when both partners freely communicate their needs.

Open sexual communication doesn't just happen. Having not heard sex talked about openly while we were growing up, most of us feel uncomfortable verbalizing our sexual concerns. Besides, we women are quite sure that if our husbands really loved us, they would know what we need—right, ladies? As some women have lamented to me, "But, Mrs. Mayo, if I had to *tell* him what I wanted it wouldn't be romantic!"

Good sex is the result of being on the same wavelength through healthy communication. If we feel loved, if our concerns have been heard and considered, if we are in touch with our partner mentally as well as physically, sexual fulfillment will come naturally. Talking about a mutual problem, working together on a project, playing together, or sharing your dreams initiates the warm feelings needed to be sexually responsive. Both men and women need this sharing, but women find it even more crucial to their ability to respond sexually.

Commitment. As Christians, we are fortunate to have God's commitment to love us and never abandon us in spite of our shortcomings. What a model for commitment in our marriages! Knowing that we do not have the option of deserting our spouses is a great motivator for improving the existing union. The life and health of your marriage and family depend on your commitment to make your marriage what it was designed to be. It is a researched fact that husbands and wives who take their commitment to the Lord and to each other seriously have greater sexual satisfaction.[1]

Mutual commitment also gives us the freedom to take risks and to make mistakes. For example, let's say that one night you decide to lay all your inhibitions aside and be the ultimate lover to your husband. But instead of oohing and aahing when you slink out of the bathroom, he laughs because you inadvertently put your new silk gown on inside out. If you are truly committed to each other, such embarrassments won't damage your marriage or dampen your sexual appetites. Committed couples can laugh at themselves one minute and be deeply romantic the next.

Compromise. Compromise is not the same as sacrifice because both parties get as much as possible of what they want. What we both want in marriage is, of course, a strong and secure union. Nothing else has more influence on our kids.

But forging a strong union through compromise is a continuing process that requires a lot of time. You must plan special times for communication. You must commit yourself to making your relationship a priority, even above the kids.

For example, my husband and I have explained to our children since they were little that a good relationship for Dad and Mom requires that we spend time alone without them. They understand that we will go out on dates that exclude them and retire to our bedroom for private times. Without quality time together you can't hammer out the compromises that are essential to a healthy marriage and sexual relationship.

The ARA Formula for Women

Here's my formula for a fulfilling sexual relationship: Good Sex = Arousal + Relaxation + Assertiveness. No formula is foolproof, but this is a good one because it encompasses all the elements we have discussed in this chapter.

Arousal. You cannot be maximally aroused unless you are mentally comfortable with your partner, yourself, and your physical surroundings (such as a private room). Being mentally comfortable includes a decent degree of self-esteem, for without it we fail to believe we deserve or are capable of giving pleasure. Mental comfort also means that you see sex as good and that you are sure you are functioning within God's guidelines.

In counseling people with low sexual desires, my husband and I frequently liken sexual arousal to a pot of boiling water on the stove. If the water is cold, it takes a long time for it to heat up to the boiling point. Likewise, arousal may take a long time after a hard day. If, however, the pot is kept on simmer all day, the critical temperature is reached more quickly. Obviously, if sexual thoughts and plans are kept in mind during the day, getting into a sexual mood in the evening will be more easily accomplished.

Relaxation. As mentioned earlier, sexual arousal and fulfillment depend on a healthy, relaxed body, the result of good exercise, good nutrition, and adequate rest. You don't have to be taught how to respond sexually; it's an innate, God-given ability. You simply need to be relaxed enough to maximize the conditions for doing what comes naturally.

Assertiveness. In order to be sexually fulfilled, you need to be bold enough to tell your partner what you want and need. Many women have difficulty being sexually assertive, thinking that their husbands will automatically know what they want. But think about your other appetites. Do you expect your husband to know what you want for dinner every night or what you would like for a birthday gift? Of course not. Yet he is expected to be a mindreader when it comes to your sexual appetite. Why continue being hurt when he guesses wrong? Give the poor fellow a clue! If you are clear about what your needs are and ask for them to be met, there is a good chance you will get what you want.

Questions Women Ask about Sexual Fulfillment

I think sex is very overrated. Why don't I enjoy it?

There are many reasons a woman may not enjoy sex. If sexual activities are not mutually agreed upon, sex can be a miserable, frightening, or demeaning experience. That's why sex in the New Testament is described in terms of mutuality instead of dominance.

Sometimes sex is not enjoyable because past sexual experiences with other partners contaminate its meaning and purpose in your marriage. You need to rid yourself of these "ghosts" with the help of a competent pastor or counselor, especially in the case of sexual abuse.

You may not enjoy sex because you're comparing your experience with the fantasy model presented in the media. Few husbands are as consistently romantic and tender as your favorite leading man appears to be on the screen. And no couple experiences a dramatic, room-shaking, simultaneous orgasm every time as lovers seem to in the movies. The key to enjoyable sex is having a positive attitude about each other even when an anticipated love scene fizzles instead of sizzles.

If feeling turned-off sexually is something new for you, it may be the result of a communication breakdown. Perhaps you're focusing on having sex instead of on making love and knowing one another. Talking about your sex life is important because it increases the chance that you will get what you desire, enjoy sex more, and feel close and intimate.

If you are not enjoying sex, schedule a physical checkup to eliminate any biological causes. Also take an honest look at your lifestyle. Are there new stressors? Are you tired? Are you depressed? Are you failing to see your spouse as a blessing or to hold him in high regard? All of these can take the fun out of sex for you.

My husband wants me to wear sexy lingerie. How does God feels about this?

In His wisdom, God did not include in the Bible a list of 201 dos and don'ts for the bedroom. He is obviously more concerned about His purpose and design for sex being achieved— joy, pleasure, bonding, and sometimes a new life—than about our sticking to a prepackaged lovemaking plan.

In Song of Songs a husband and wife search for new places to make love; verbalize their sexual likes, wants, and needs; and strive to please each other sexually. This biblical wife not only performs an erotic dance for her husband (6:13–8:4)—a thought that terrorizes my lead feet—but attracts him by using lipstick and rouge (4:3), wearing jewelry (4:9) and perfume (4:10), and donning a see-through negligee (4:5,11).

Research has verified repeatedly that men are sexually aroused through physical and visible stimuli—like your husband seeing you in sexy lingerie! God designed him that way, just as he designed you to be aroused through romance and relationship. Within the parameters of what you are comfortable with, stretch yourself to appeal to your husband in the ways God equipped him to be aroused.

How can I avoid hurting my husband's feelings when I tell him I don't want to make love?

If your husband asks you to play tennis and you say no, chances are it doesn't bother him! But the male ego is so intertwined with his sexuality that it's difficult for him to take a turn-down gracefully.

It is important for your husband to understand that unless you give him an honest no you can't give him an honest yes.

Does your husband view lovemaking as the only way he can express love or be intimate with you? Is intercourse proof to him that you love him? Sometimes people need assurance that closeness and love can be expressed in other ways.

If you both wanted something different for dinner, I'll bet you could come up with a compromise that pleased you both. Continuing to verbalize what you need sexually will result in a creative compromise that works for both of you. The biggest danger is allowing differences in desire or timing to turn sex into a power play instead of a mutually loving experience.

What should I share with my daughter about sex and sexuality?

It is essential that you encourage your daughter to know and be comfortable with her own body and its sexual function. This is important for two reasons. First, it's a matter of good health. If she grows up familiar with her normal body state, as an adult she can confidently share with her doctor any changes that appear suspicious. Second, by knowing her body your daughter will be more comfortable sharing her sexual needs with her future husband.

Your daughter needs to know that her contribution to life includes her God-designed feminine perspective, and that she need not deny it, apologize for it, or feel limited by it. To ignore that her unique muscularity, physiology, and genetic balance affects the way she perceives life is very shortsighted. Research continues to verify her special difference as a female, particularly when it comes to valuing and being sensitive to relationships.[2]

Finally, you must model for your daughter the value a woman should place on herself and her future husband. How do you convey through your behavior that you hold the same high opinion of yourself that God holds? What behavior communicates that you honor and respect your husband even though he isn't perfect? Such attitudes and actions modeled by you are essential if your daughter is to develop and function sexually in a healthy manner.

5

For Dad (and the Woman in His Life)

Mr. Smith's frail body was draped limply over a chair in the doctor's office as he awaited the diagnosis. Mrs. Smith sat prim and proper in the chair next to him.

Dr. Antonio looked at Mr. Smith over the rim of his half-glasses with the gravest expression he could muster. "Mr. Smith, you are in terrible shape. Unless you get lots of home cooking and good sex, you are going to die."

Mr. Smith suddenly showed signs of life. "Edith, did you hear that?"

Mrs. Smith's stoic expression was unchanged. "Yes, Dear," she responded without hesitation. "The doctor said you are going to die."

Contrary to all the myths and jokes, both men and women have the capacity to enjoy sex. Since the woman's response is affected by so many factors, she is often labeled as being less interested in sex than the man. Rarely will a man admit that at times he doesn't feel like having sex.

Dad, your sexuality, sexual relationship with your wife, and communication about sex is as much a part of your children's sex education as that of their mother. You may not have as many opportunities to talk to your children about sex, but your example of positive sexuality in the home will either validate or invalidate what you do say. This chapter will help you understand the male sexual system and provide guidelines for your sexual relationship with the mother of your children.

Becoming the World's Authority on You

As with females, men have both internal and external organs for sex and reproduction. Working from outside to inside, let's make sure you understand your sexual organs and their functions.

The External Male Organs

The *penis* contains many blood vessels and nerves. It consists of three concentric, sponge-like cylinders that fill with blood during arousal to cause an erection. There is no muscle or bone in the human penis. That's why a male cannot simply will an erection. It must be allowed to happen.

The penis is attached to the pelvis at the *root*. The free portion of the penis is called the *body*. The smooth tip is known as the *glans*. The glans is by far the most sensitive area of the penis, particularly the underside where a little ridge of skin called the *frenulum* lies. The urethral opening, the *meatus*, can be seen at the very tip. The glans and the body meet at the neck of the penis where an excess of skin, some of which folds over and covers the glans, forms the *foreskin*.

In Judeo-Christian tradition, the foreskin is often surgically removed, a procedure called circumcision. Besides its early religious significance, circumcision has proved to be a health benefit to both men and women. Here in the United States where circumcision is almost universally performed, men have a much lower rate of cancer of the penis, and wives whose husbands are circumcised have lower rates of cervical cancer.

The average penis is three to four inches long in a non-erect (flaccid) state and slightly over six inches long when erect.

There is nothing advantageous about an exceptionally large penis, especially when you remember that the most sensitive areas for a woman are external or no more than two inches within the vagina.

In contrast to the hairless penis, the *scrotal sac* or *scrotum* has some hair and many sweat glands. Muscle fibers enable the sac to react involuntarily to cold temperatures, sexual excitement, and other stimuli.

The Internal Male Organs

The *scrotum* contains two compartments, each housing a *testicle* (or *testis*) and its *spermatic cord*. The cord suspends the testicle and carries the *vas deferens* which transport sperm from the testicle into the pelvic cavity. There the vas deferens join the seminal vesicle duct to form the ejaculatory duct, continuing through the prostate and into the *urethra*.

The urethra carries semen and urine, but never at the same time. During sexual excitement, urine flow is blocked by a valve, and the *bulbourethral glands* (Cowper's glands) release a clear liquid that neutralizes the acid in the canal in preparation for the passage of sperm. Sperm may be present in this discharge, which explains why pregnancy occasionally occurs from sexual contact even without ejaculation.

The *seminal vesicles* supply a small amount of fluid that is thought to mobilize the sperm. The prostate itself supplies most of the seminal fluid and its characteristic odor. It is easy to see how enlargement of the prostate—a common problem in older men—causes difficulty in urination, since the urethra runs right through it.

Like the ovaries, the male testicles or testes have two functions: producing the male hormone testosterone and producing sperm for reproduction. Testes are slightly larger than female ovaries. It is not unusual for the left testicle to hang slightly lower than the right to keep them from rubbing together uncomfortably when men walk.

Each testicle consists of a number of lobes filled with threadlike structures called *seminiferous tubules*. It is here that sperm are produced and begin to mature. The tubules of

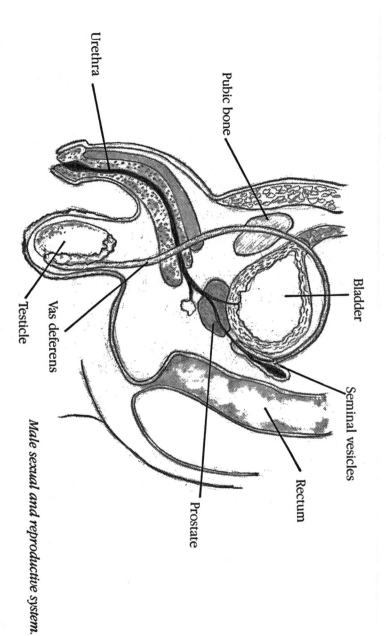

Urethra

Pubic bone

Bladder

Seminal vesicles

Rectum

Prostate

Vas deferens

Testicle

Male sexual and reproductive system.

an infant are solid. During puberty they develop a hollow center through which sperm will pass.

A Man's Sexual Response

Internal and external changes take place in the male during sexual excitement. The beginning of an erection is the first response. If stimulation is sustained, a "point of inevitability" will be reached when ejaculation (the release of the semen) occurs involuntarily. There is no equivalent phenomenon of inevitability for women.

Since a man so closely associates ejaculation and the accompanying orgasm with a complete act, he often has difficulty accepting the idea that sex can be fulfilling with or without this one aspect. The sexual "stud," who often functions well physically but finds his sexual relationships empty, is evidence of the consequences of this wrong thinking.

Besides erection, the man will also notice testicular elevation, body flushes, generalized muscle tension, and all the other bodily responses aroused women experience. After ejaculation, a period of time must pass before a man can experience another erection and orgasm. Women, however, can experience multiple orgasms in a short period of time.

As a man ages, he may find that the time required between his erections increases. He may also notice that the nature of sexual stimulation must be very direct and involve more time. In his youth the mere sight of his wife preparing for bed was stimulus enough. Such changes do not reflect a diminished affection. A recent survey on old age and sex stated that, although sex was performed less frequently (but with greater frequency than you might imagine!), it was more satisfying than earlier in life.

Guidelines for Good Sex

An 86-year-old man came to see a colleague of my husband for a checkup. During the examination the old gentleman mentioned rather casually that he had recently become impotent.

"Are you concerned about this?" the physician inquired with sensitivity.

"No, I haven't thought too much about it," the old man replied. "I'm sure it's just a delayed reaction to the saltpeter I received during World War I."

How many men would handle a similar crisis with such aplomb! A less self-assured husband might panic at the first sign of malfunction, then scurry to the bookstore for a sex manual on 1001 new positions. He also may have some suggestions for his wife, whom he will probably blame for the problem: dress up for dinner, lose weight, buy a sexy nightie. Finally he may resort to having an affair in order to jump-start his engine and prove to himself that the old machinery still works.

Men, there is much more to a fulfilling sexual relationship than new positions and sexy nighties. As an alternative to the panic reaction above, I suggest you focus on implementing the three R's, the three C's, and the ARA formula as they apply to your sexual relationship with your wife.

The Three R's for Men

Response. A man's panic reaction to sexual difficulties rarely includes the question, "Do I really want sex tonight?" After all, men are always ready, willing, and able for sex, right? Wrong. That's a myth of male sexuality. Women may be at fault for not giving enough thought to their sexuality. Men err at the other end of the continuum—tending to exaggerate the importance of sex in their lives. For men, any hint of sexual disinterest or dysfunction is wrongly attributed monumental significance as the beginning of a downward spiral to impotence.

This exaggeration is one of many myths which have grown from widespread sexual ignorance among men. The average man gets most of his sexual information from other men who know as little as he knows. There must be 30 books on female sexuality to every one on male sexuality. (I highly recommend the book *Male Sexuality* [Bantam] by Bernie Zilbergeld. This is not a Christian book, but the information on male sexual response is excellent.)

Men need to understand that sexual response is as much a choice for them as it is for women and that it's okay sometimes *not* to respond.

Relaxation. Little attention has been given to the fact that men, like women, respond according to their moods and feelings. Their sexual response is subject to all the pressures that affect any of their other natural functions. In a world that measures a man by the amount of money he earns, who has time to relax long enough for meaningful sex?

The need to perform permeates all aspects of a man's life, including sex. In counseling I have found few men who are in touch with what they emotionally and physically want from sexual sharing. It takes a great deal of attention and assurance to get a man to the point where he can admit he is too tired for sex. Perhaps he would just like to hold his wife.

But that isn't sex, you say. Sure it is! Sex is whatever meets you and your partner's needs and results in a feeling of sharing and closeness. But you won't discover these joys until you physically and mentally relax.

Respect. Men, if you want your wife to contribute to your personal and sexual fulfillment, you must contribute to hers by respecting her as a woman and valuing her role in your home highly. Give her that extra mile of support and appreciation for all she does for you and your family. Let her see your commitment to treasure the home as she does.

You also respect your wife by taking care of yourself. Remember the "for better or for worse" part of your vow? A number of men seem to think it means the wife must always be better (better looking, better educated, better mother, better lover, etc.) while the husband is allowed to be worse (fatter, out of shape, less romantic, narrower in interest, etc.). The "for better" refers to you too!

Respect for your wife also requires that you discern her unique lovemaking style. One man came into the counseling office very upset. "I'm here because my wife has a problem. I've tried everything to please her sexually. I'm well read on all the latest techniques. I know about foreplay, I fondle her breasts …"

"I never liked that," his wife interrupted, her voice trailing off.

"What?"

"I said I never liked my breasts fondled."

"But the book said you would love it!"

"I don't care what your book says, I've never enjoyed it."

"Well, what do you want?"

"How about roses!"

Finally, you respect your wife by nurturing her spiritually. What are you doing to present your wife "without blemish" to the Lord as you are asked to do in Ephesians 5:26? Are you helping her become the woman God intended her to be? What unique traits, skills, and propensities does your wife have that need to be encouraged and nurtured? As you respect her by caring for her in these ways, you will reap dividends in your sexual relationship.

The Three C's for Men

Communication. A friend once confided to me that her husband desired intercourse daily and sometimes twice a day. But when she requested him to say he loved her, he couldn't understand it. After all, he "showed" his love to her every day!

It is difficult for most men to talk about sex. Nonverbal love messages are important and can be quite communicative, but they have their limitations. Men, your wives need your loving words as well as your loving deeds.

Some men fear the intimacy of conversation. They have been taught to equate personal sharing with vulnerability and vulnerability with weakness. Ironically, when the people we love know all about us, they generally love us more. When you let your wife know through your open sharing that you are human and fallible, she can risk being herself with you. Being willing to be vulnerable through sharing is a path to a fulfilling relationship.

Communication is threatening to some men who are afraid of hurting their wives by telling the truth. It took my husband eight years to tell me it drove him crazy when I didn't get the last drop of toothpaste out of the sink after I brushed. Each morning his stress level rose over something I could have easily changed if he had only told me about it. The Bible tells us to admonish those who are wrong, but to wrap our reproof in love. Most irritants between couples are willingly removed if they are pointed out in a spirit of love and respect.

We are also afraid of disagreeing with our spouses. The prevailing myth is that people in love will always want the same things. Differences are seen as the end of the marriage. But we are complex, independent beings. We need to agree on the "biggies": the role of Christ in our lives, our basic lifestyle, the role of children. But the rest is open to differing opinions. Having differences is not really the problem; how we express our differences is more likely the basis of trouble.

One way to improve communication with your wife is by using "I-language" in your sexual sharing. Take responsibility for your statements by using sentences that begin with "I" instead of with "you," "we," or "let's." For example, you-language sounds like this:

> He: Would you like to make love tonight?
> She: I don't know, would you?
> He: Whatever you want pleases me.
> She: I just want you to be happy.

But I-language sounds like this:

> He: I feel very romantic tonight. I'd like to go up to the bedroom right now.
> She: I'm very tired. I'd like to take a relaxing bath first.
> He: That's fine with me.

Here are a few more tips for using I-language:
- Avoid words like "ought," "should," and "have to," and substitute "might," "could," and "I want to."
- Don't use questions to mask what you are really saying. For example, "Why are you mad?" often means "I'm

feeling that you are angry and I need to check that out with you."

- Don't use the words "always" and "never." Try "up until now" or "in the past." For example, instead of "You always want sex when I've had a bad day," try "Up until now, it seems you feel like having sex on days that are difficult for me."
- Throw out "I don't know" and "I don't care." You *do* care—you just may not care very strongly.

Commitment and *Compromise.* The information in Chapter 4 on these topics applies here as well. Without commitment and compromise, you will have difficulty making much of anything work in your marriage, particularly sexual fulfillment.

The ARA Formula for Men

Let's focus on some specific applications of the ARA formula (Good Sex = Arousal + Relaxation + Assertiveness) for men.

Arousal. A major male myth is that all physical contact between husband and wife must lead to sex. The awful result is that most touching between the spouses ceases because they are not always ready, willing, or able to go the distance. After a period of no touching, they begin to feel alienated. And when alienation occurs, arousal is even more remote.

Touch must not always be regarded as the trigger for intercourse; it is an end in itself. My touch component is such that if my husband and I don't spend some time just sitting together in the evening, I feel out of balance. I am sure a few of you are thinking, "I don't need touch. I don't even like it." You *do* need it. If arousal through touching is difficult for you or your spouse, embark on a training program to awaken this aspect of your relationship. Start slowly, perhaps with foot or hand massages, and resensitize—or desensitize!—as needed.

Arousal is also negatively affected when the naturalness of sexual response is ignored. "You must have a sexual appetite because I do" or "Sex can be good only if you have an orgasm exactly when I do" are demands that stifle arousal. Would you insist on someone eating apple pie because that is what you craved? Silly, you say? You bet it is. As silly as insisting on the same degree of arousal or simultaneous orgasms.

Relaxation. Two other male myths fit in this category. The first we have already alluded to: Sex equals intercourse. On the contrary, good sex is whatever meets our needs and our partner's needs at any given time. This relaxed attitude can be extremely freeing and consequently very arousing. A preconceived notion of what makes the experience successful does more to work against success than anything else I can think of. Relax and let sex be sex, with or without intercourse.

Here's another detrimental male myth that must be eliminated: Sex can only happen with an erection. The primary cause of impotency is worrying about impotency. The male will probably never have a problem if he accepts that both he and his partner can derive pleasure whether or not he has an erect penis.

Assertiveness. By using I-language and responding accordingly you will probably get what you want sexually. But you may worry that such assertiveness will ruin the spontaneity of sex. I personally know of few things that are actually better for spontaneity than direct communication and planning.

A scheduled gourmet meal is enjoyable because you have anticipated the special time and place and have fantasized about the carefully planned menu. But that doesn't mean you can't be spontaneous at the table—eating foods from your plate in whatever order you like, going back for seconds, etc. Similarly, you plan the time and the setting for sex, but you don't schedule the interlude minute by minute. You don't plan what position(s) will be most enjoyable or how each of you will respond. That's where creative spontaneity takes over.

Consider what is involved in actualizing a spontaneous sexual experience. Both you and your partner's natural response systems must be working at the same level. You must be rested. You must not be distracted by business or household chores. The weather in the meadow must be balmy (the location must be suitable!). And little Joey must go to bed on time, not need any water or extra prayers, and have his favorite teddy bear handy. Good luck!

Questions Men Ask About Sexual Fulfillment

My wife claims she can enjoy sex with or without an orgasm. I can't relate to that. Is it true, or is she just trying to make me feel better?

Is sexual fulfillment the same for men and women? None of us can know for sure! You can only be the world's authority on what feels right or good to you. However, it's true that women seem to appreciate and need the "ambiance" of sex more than men do. As physically focused as a man is, it is difficult for him to imagine that a physical response may not be the measure of his wife's pleasure. Chances are that when you get older you will have times when coitus will end without ejaculation. This is a natural phenomenon that occurs with aging. I guarantee that you will enjoy the experience anyway. Sexual health involves the freedom to respond or not as one desires. Sex is good because of the totality of the relationship.

If your wife never has an orgasm, I advise the two of you to read some of the excellent books available on the subject, such as *Becoming Orgasmic: A Sexual Growth Program for Women* (Prentice-Hall), by J. Heiman, L. LoPiccolo, and J. LoPiccolo.

I enjoy oral sex and so does my wife, but she always feels guilty afterward. Why?

Every individual has personal sexual preferences, interpretations of Scripture regarding sex, and past learning experiences that include and preclude certain sexual practices. These need to be heeded. Couples are to share their bodies in ways that they mutually agree upon and that make them both feel bonded, healthy, and physically pleasured. Each couple must work out together what brings them closer sexually. It is wrong for one partner to force anything the other partner is uncomfortable with.

At the same time, the depiction of married love in Song of Songs shows each partner stretching to meet the needs of the other in a way that is meaningful and significant to them. Research tells us that couples who vary their sexual repertoire, particularly as they get older, have the happiest and most satisfying sex lives. It's okay for you to patiently encourage your wife to stretch in some areas if you are equally willing to stretch in order to accommodate her comfort zone.

We sometimes enjoy using sexual "toys" when we make love. Is there anything wrong with these additions?

Many couples employ a variety of stimulation devices such as vibrators, games such as "An Enchanted Evening" and healthy romantic movies or stories (not pornography), or poetry to energize their sex life. It's part of human nature to be curious and to experiment. Scripture tells us that nothing is bad if it is received with thanksgiving, but some things are not beneficial (1 Timothy 4:4,5; 1 Corinthians 6:12).

I have two cautions. First, no toy or ritual should become so necessary to your lovemaking that you can never get aroused or fulfilled without it. Sometimes we opt for these shortcuts to performance-based fulfillment instead of persevering through the sometimes tedious, discouraging soul-searching and relationship-building needed for sexual intimacy. The focus of marital love is the relationship, not a marathon of ever-increasing physical experiences.

Second, books, videos, or activities that sexually arouse us to people other than our spouse are clearly not Scriptural. Our erotic fantasy life is to be limited to our partner (Matthew 5:27,28). It is on this issue that you find the greatest difference between secular and Christian sex counseling.

All the books talk about women not wanting sex. In our home I'm the one who is less interested. Why doesn't sex seem worth the effort anymore?

This man may be suffering from the number one sexual problem: inhibited sexual desire (ISD). It seems strange that in a sex-focused society our greatest sexual problem is not wanting to be sexual!

If you find your sexual desire waning, it is wise to have a thorough physical exam and an evaluation of your medications to see if there is a physiological explanation. Then obvious stressors such as unresolved relationship issues, job pressures, overwork, and fatigue all need to be considered and dealt with. Sometimes it is necessary to examine and resolve past sexual experiences, especially if they were forced, manipulative, or shameful.

Take note of thought patterns you employ that tend to shut the door to your sexual desires. For example, you may think of your wife lovingly while you're at the office and even after you get home. But as soon as you prepare for bed and the possibility of sex arises, you find yourself thinking of her negatively: dinner wasn't what you wanted, her hips are getting too wide, her new haircut makes her look like a boy, she has nothing interesting to say. I call this "turn-off thinking." By the time you get into bed you can hardly stand to be in the same room with her, let alone make love to her. Sound familiar?

ISD is difficult for therapists to treat because the causes are often complex, overlapping, and sometimes subconscious. I suggest the following steps for dealing with your inhibited sexual desire:

1. Confess to God that your lack of desire is sinful and that you want to be the husband God intended you to be.

2. Ask God to help you find people, books, and the courage to face the issues that are contributing to your behavior.

3. Communicate with your wife your sincere desire to change, and elicit her cooperation and patience. Keep the communication lines open as you gain insight.

4. Share with your wife specific ways she can help you.

5. Focus on the internal turn-offs you use to decrease your desire. When do they start? Can you recognize a pattern?

6. Put a stop to your turn-off thinking by renewing your mind (Romans 12:2). Substitute an appropriate Scripture or positive statement prepared beforehand every time your turn-off thinking begins.

7. If renewing your sexual relationship seems especially threatening, take your time and go slow. Give each other permission to touch and hold without intercourse. Take baths or showers together. Give each other massages. Progress to more intimate touching only when it seems comfortable and right for both of you.

8. Never try to make love when you are physically or mentally stressed, angry, or distracted. Maximize your physical environment. Does music help? Are the kids likely to barge in? Pay attention to externals and the conditions that maximize your desire.

9. Like Solomon in Song of Songs, learn to give your wife a blessing. If this is a difficult concept for you, read *The Blessing* (Thomas Nelson) and *The Language of Love* (Word) by Gary Smalley and John Trent.

What should I share with my son about sex and sexuality?

The most important message a father can convey to his son is an accurate definition of manhood—and it has little to do with sexual intercourse. He needs to know that a real man's life is not run by his hormones. A real man cherishes and respects women, values them as partners, and is capable of self-discipline and self-control.

Are you subconsciously encouraging your son to view and pursue girls as sex objects? Are the traits you are reinforcing in him only of the "macho" variety? Does your son know that you consider him a man even if he doesn't play sports and sleeps with a computer? How often do you verbalize your approval of the attributes that indicate he is growing into a man of God? Society is screaming at him to act on his sexuality. Can he hear your voice above the din?

It is essential that your son learn to verbalize his sexual desires, fears, and questions. With your positive example, he no longer needs to tolerate ignorance based on his reluctance to talk about sex for fear of appearing unmanly. Your modeling of open and clear communication techniques about sex is a gift to him of irreplaceable value.

What about "Daddy's little girl?" What is my responsibility for my daughter's sexual development?

Few fathers understand the significance of their influence on their daughters' budding sexuality. If you are erratic in nurturing her, or if you pull away from her and the family physically or emotionally, she is likely to have difficulty adjusting sexually to her future husband, particularly when it comes to experiencing orgasm. Lesbian women often have abusive fathers in their background.

If, however, you affirm her femininity and her right to be different from her mother, and if you dependably care for her and her mother, she is more apt to be sexually responsive with her husband. It is through you that she will learn to trust men. As the first man in her life, you hold the key to her successful interaction with all the other men she will relate to in her lifetime.

PART 2

Your Child
and
"The Facts"

6

The Preschool Child

Jerry's red hair shone like a halo in the sunlight flowing through the car's sunroof. Of all her children, Kathryn thought, Jerry reflected a love of life that made her occasionally wish she could freeze time and continue to bask in his exuberance. He was always bursting with information when she picked him up from playschool. In five minutes she had already heard about Mrs. Diamond's new cat (she promised to bring it next Thursday), Amy's fall out of the swing (she cried), and Joel's boast of counting to 500 (he lies).

The litany of playschool news was capped, however, by Jerry's declaration that he and Mary Lou were both pregnant! "Do you know what it means to be pregnant?" Kathryn asked, trying to sound nonchalant. She couldn't believe she was talking to her three-year-old baby about sex.

"Oh yes, Mom. It means you can write with both hands!" Kathryn carefully corrected her suddenly teachable son. "Mom," he said after her brief explanation, "Mary Lou and I are *not* pregnant."

Before we launch into several chapters written to help you talk to your Jerry or Mary Lou about "pregnant" and other topics related to sex and sexuality, we'd better decide what sex education is. In 1975 the World Health Organization determined that sexual health is "the integration of the physical, emotional, intellectual and social aspects of sexual beings in ways that are positively enriching and that enhance personality, communication and love."[1] Not bad! But I think there's more to it. Sex education is helping your children learn to *give* as well as *feel* warmth and love. It's helping them understand and integrate their sexual identity. It's helping them develop positive self-concepts. All of these elements enable your children to make responsible and moral decisions regarding their physical, mental, emotional, and social selves. The technical side of sex education is not to be overlooked, but sex education is a lot more than sperm, eggs, and positions! Beyond reproduction we are teaching values and identity.

Furthermore, in a world that exposes a new case of child sexual abuse hourly, we must also instill in our children a sense of "my body, under my control, inviolate." Sexual exploitation can take a multitude of forms. For many it does not end with childhood, but continues into dating and marriage. Special issues of sex education such as sexual abuse will be discussed more fully in the last two chapters.

A Time to Learn, a Time to Teach

As news got out that I was writing a book about children and sexuality, the number one question I heard was, "When do you suggest we start talking to our kids about sex, when they turn 12?" When I glibly replied, "Day one," I'm sure many dismissed me as mad or secretly perverted! But day one is none too soon to begin because, whether you like it or not, your child's basic concept of sex and sexuality will be formed by age five. No, he probably won't be able to diagram the reproductive system or describe the dynamics of foreplay and intercourse. But he will have assimilated your attitude about sex from how you respond to his sexual behaviors and questions. And everything he hears about sex from then on will be filtered through the attitude he has picked up from you and your example.

Sex education must also begin on day one because kids are natural-born explorers. When little Cynthia takes apart an old clock or Toby removes all the screws from the kitchen cabinets, we (after the initial shock) proudly affirm their curiosity, ingenuity, and willingness to learn. Then we hasten to provide more acceptable outlets for their interests.

However, when their summer project is discovering the difference between boys and girls by means of a lab conducted in the backyard, our tolerance for the scientific method comes to a screeching halt. But does it make sense that their method for learning about body parts through exploration would be any different from their method for learning about clocks and screwdrivers? I'm not saying that more acceptable outlets for their curiosity needn't be found. I'm simply saying that it is normal for young children to investigate their sexual differences, so you'd better be ready to talk about them.

Too Much or Too Little?

We shy away from talking to our young children about sex because we fear that they will become sexually aware and active too early. But you can rest assured that you will not harm your children by sharing too much. A child's sexual curiosity is easily satiated. When their little minds have absorbed all they can handle, they are quickly diverted to other interests. For example, our four-year-old Joey's first sex education book, *Where Did I Come From?* made very little impression on him. After what I thought was our most thorough discussion on sexuality to date, I asked Joey if he had any questions. "Yes," he replied. "May I go watch cartoons now?"

Your real concern should be explaining too little about sex. I am not suggesting that a child be exposed to pornography, the details of explicit sexual acts, or your sexual life. But general sexual information will not cause irreparable shock or motivate your child to become the little Don (or Donna) Juan of the neighborhood. In fact, well-informed children are less likely to involve themselves in sexual situations.

Sexual ideas and exploration are a part of every child's life.

It's not sex education that makes them curious about penises, vaginas, breasts, and where babies come from. God is responsible for that, because that's how He made them. As in any other part of life, our goal for our children's sex education should be for them to know, to understand, and to gain mastery.

The Infant: The Original Bon Vivant

The infant makes no apology for the fact that his or her world is one of sensual delight. He thrives on touch, smell, and warm, wet nourishment. Whether life will be good or bad is reduced to how dependably these treasures are supplied. The infant who is denied them fails to develop normally. The infant whose needs are met irregularly learns that the world is a scary place where you can trust no one.

Exploration and Arousal

Infants are often sexually aroused during diaper changes. I encourage you not to deliberately stimulate your infant, but allow normal contact that stimulates arousal (cleansing the genitals, applying powder or lotion, etc.). We can only guess at the anger, resistance, and frustration that might surface in the child by blocking biologically authentic feelings.

Allowing infants the freedom to enjoy and explore themselves need not be frightening to us. It is just one part of a child's ever-expanding world. While this is an important part of the sensuous world of the infant, I guarantee it won't continue to be his or her major occupation.

Erotic feelings are not experienced only by the infant. With the fluctuation of hormones after birth and the intimate contact involved in caring for the child, mothers are particularly subject to arousal. Accepting this phenomenon as normal and, in a sense, as a sign of bonding and closeness is the mature approach.

Acceptance does not mean giving free rein to such feelings, however. You must acknowledge them and determine what you will do with them without allowing any gesture to become sexualized. For example, a peck on the mouth is different from a kiss that involves the tongue, and bathing should involve the whole child, not just his or her genital area. If you are fearful of erring in the appropriateness of touch, always err in the direction of affection rather than pulling away.

Swimming is a healthy way to allow children to enjoy their bodies and the closeness of others. Most towns have parent-infant classes that purport to make children water safe. More important, however, when infants play in the water with few or no clothes on, they learn to be at ease with the way they look, smell, move, and feel. It is through such an experience that we can begin to teach a significant message, namely that certain behaviors are proper only in specific settings.

It is during infancy that you should begin referring to body parts—including genitals—by their proper names. Why start before a child can even talk? First, it desensitizes the parents so they are comfortable when the child asks for the first time, "What's that for?" Second, the child grows up with no guilt attached to parts that have been considered nameless or unmentionable. Since no body part has been excluded or touted above another, he can accept his whole body in a healthy way.

Finally, we need to consider the matter of where an infant sleeps. If there is any other alternative, a baby should not be in the parents' room. We don't know when they are able to perceive aggression, but we know that infants are upset when the sights and/or sounds of lovemaking cause them to fear that Mother is being hurt. Furthermore, the sound of a baby's sweet gurgle makes it difficult for you to concentrate on being your husband's femme fatale or your wife's knight in shining armor!

The Terrific Two's and Three's

Two- and three-year-olds embody all the elements that make them ideally teachable. They are naturally curious and hungry for facts. Most of all, they accept their parents as the "masters of the universe." They will take what you say literally and believe it wholeheartedly simply because you said it. (Enjoy this stage; it won't happen again!)

Discovering the Differences

As during the infant stage, proper names for body parts are essential. A penis is a penis. The equivalent for the female at this stage is the vulva, for the vulva, unlike the clitoris or vagina, can be seen. And what is seen is important, as two-year-old Jeffrey understood. Sitting on his potty chair while his older sister Lauren was perched on the toilet, Jeffrey said in his proudest voice, "Mommy, Jeffrey has penis; you don't. You and Lauren need to go to market and get penis." It is safe to assume that Jeffrey had a pretty good body image, although we can only guess how Lauren felt!

Young children, although hampered in their understanding of emotion, are quick to pick up the distinction of "I'm a boy" or "I'm a girl." In fact, one of the major developmental tasks for this age is establishing the child's gender.

There are many ways to assure this process. Young children should be allowed to dress and take baths together and talk with you about the differences they notice. Watching animals give birth is usually an excellent time to point out many facts about birth and for introducing the different meaning sex has for animals and people.

A new baby in the home is another wonderful source of information. Inspections should preferably take place with a parent's help and approval. Discussing the baby's parts together will relieve the toddler's anxiety about his or her own sex. More important, you will be seen as a source of information and demonstrate that you are askable even about sexual organs and functions. Be truthful. Ask your child if he understands. Tell him you will be available to talk again. After several inspections, the toddler's interest will shift to other new and exciting discoveries.

When talking to your toddler about sex, talk about people instead of birds, bees, and flowers. Children at this age need specifics. They can't connect bees pollinating flowers and spiders laying eggs with human reproduction. Similes like these only confuse the child as he struggles to assure himself that Mommy will not sting Daddy to death after mating like the black widow spider does.

Clean or Dirty?

Since the excretory and sex organs are so close, be careful to distinguish between them. Many children become confused during potty training when we communicate about germs and the necessity of wiping properly and cleaning our hands. It is easy to see why sex organs are thought of as dirty and untouchable if a distinction to the contrary hasn't been made.

Young Susan didn't have any such problem. Her potty training was progressing well, but Susan still needed her mother's help in cleaning herself. One day her mother casually commented, "Let me clean your crack, Susan."

"My crack? Am I broken, Mommy?" Susan replied with alarm.

Susan's mother carefully explained that "crack" was a slang word and that she was not broken. "Well, 'crack' sounds nasty," Susan protested.

"What would you prefer that we call it?" asked a very anxious-to-please mother.

"Let's call it 'Priscilla,'" came the quick response. Priscilla was a dearly loved friend of the family after whom Susan had named her favorite doll!

Maintain Private Times

Your children need to see you and your spouse being affectionate and happy with each other. But they should not be allowed to see you having intercourse. Privacy is essential. Always lock your door when you're being sexual. It's a message to your children that parents have private times and enjoy being alone, a fact they will tuck away for their own adulthood. You would be surprised at how many parents object to seeking privacy on grounds that their children may feel left out. A strong emotional bond between you and your spouse is the greatest assurance you can give your kids, but they don't need to invade your sexual privacy.

If a slip-up occurs and your toddler discovers you making love, stay calm. Don't pretend it didn't happen. Invite the child in to talk. Or if your position or state of arousal at the time of the "invasion" requires that you unwind first, instruct the child to go to his room and you will be there to talk to him shortly. I remember when three-year-old Malika, at keyhole height, passed by our room and got an eyeful. Her question when we later emerged from our room prompted an interesting discussion about sex: "Why was Daddy doing push-ups on the bed nude?"

Remember: A young child interprets the sounds and positions of intercourse to be aggressive. Assure him that Mommy and Daddy were doing something pleasurable, not painful. You may say, "Mommy and Daddy enjoy being alone, touching, and sharing their bodies with one another. We call it making love, and it is a very special and pleasurable time."

Your two- or three-year-old may occasionally want to join you in bed either to sleep or snuggle. As long as it is regarded an occasional, special treat and not a nightly habit, no harm is done. If, however, the child insists on coming into your room nightly, he must be made to understand that your bedroom belongs to you, not to him. It is always permissible for you to go to a child's room and rock him in a rocking chair. This way the child is reassured of your love while the special privacy between Mommy and Daddy is maintained.

The Innovative Four's and Five's

By age four or five, children should know the proper names and general functions of all parts of their bodies, including their genitals. They should also have a clear concept of which sexual topics and activities are public and which are private. They should also understand that their bodies belong to them, and that they may say no to anyone who seeks to abuse them. When children understand that sexual contact is never right unless both persons are comfortable, are of approximately equal power, and are in an appropriate setting, they will be better prepared to prevent exploitation by child molesters or a future date or spouse.

Being Touchy

It is during a child's preschool stage, sometimes as early as three, that some parents begin to reduce the amount of physical touch they give their children, particularly the boys. The idea that boys must be tough and don't need touch is wrong and harmful. The fear of producing homosexual behavior in a boy by touching him too much is unfounded. Positive physical touching is essential for mental health and building a good foundation for marriage.

Four- and five-year-olds are into touching with their peers. Sex play is rampant at this age, and there is considerable peeking and curiosity. Sex games are usually disguised, indicating that most children have gotten the message that sex is something to be shrouded in mystery or explored under other motivations. "I'll show you mine if you show me yours" is initiated as a game of daring. Playing "Doctor" or "Mommy and Daddy" is just innocent role modeling.

These exploits are realistic responses to a child's needs and sexual curiosity. Yet we almost always react negatively when we discover our four-year-old David and the little neighbor girl Sara stripped naked in the playroom giving each other impromptu physicals. Train yourself not to react negatively. Instead, count to ten, then calmly and cheerfully say to them something like, "Being curious about our bodies is healthy and normal. I have some wonderful books you would like. If you get dressed and meet me in the kitchen, I'll show you the books."

It is also perfectly permissible to close the door on the kids' sexual exploration and go on about your business. But few parents are comfortable with this solution. First because we inevitably attach adult meaning to childhood exploration and curiosity and secondly, they are concerned that Sara will later go home and entertain her parents with a blow-by-blow description of the fun she and David had playing together!

If you have overreacted to your child's sexual experimentation by shaming or punishing him or her, don't despair. Chances are a similar incident will come up, and you will be able to handle it in a more positive way. It is healthy for all concerned if you apologize when you make a mistake. Your apology, coupled with a restatement of the social manners to be expected, can set things right.

Whether or not to educate the neighbor children is a concern we all have. I have determined that if other children are around when I am educating mine, there is no harm done if they overhear. In the process they learn I am an askable adult, and I know they will only absorb what they can handle. For the same reason, I make it a habit to leave good books around the house for follow-up with neighbor children.

Having your home open to the neighborhood really helps you keep on top of where the children are emotionally with their games and whether or not healthy growth is taking place. Teaching rules for behavior in your house, while making your children aware that other homes may not have these rules, is all part of educating them.

Listen for fears and questions which arise in your children as a result of the facts you give. One little girl began to panic when she realized that her mother was soon to give birth. The mother discovered that the girl feared she would die when the baby was born because their dog died when it had too many puppies.

Crushes on Parents

Sigmund Freud has certainly dropped out of favor in some circles. But there is one area of his work that is still valid when discussing the sexuality of children: the Oedipal and Electra complexes. Frequently a five- or six-year-old daughter determines that she is going to marry her father, or a son stakes a romantic claim on his mother. How do we deal with the very real problem of cooling the ardor of an impassioned and jealous five-year-old suitor?

Although Mom and Dad need not refrain from touching each other in their child's presence, waving a red flag in front of the *petit amour* by flaunting their relationship is not right either. Rather, a father may say to his daughter positively and firmly, "I'm flattered that I am so special to you. You are special to me too, but I'm already married to your mother. Someday you will find a man who will be as important to you as I am, and that's the man you will marry." A mother can talk to her son in a similar way.

Also comment on the increasing growth and maturity you see in the child. This helps to reinforce in the child the idea that development is a continuing process and that he or she is normal. Acknowledge the child's feelings. Don't belittle him or her. And one fine day the mother/daughter and father/son rivalry will be abandoned, and the period of imitating the same-sex parent will commence.

Questions Preschool Children Ask

It is my hope that you are following the guideline of the Bible by using every opportunity to teach your children a godly perspective of life and sexuality (Deuteronomy 6:7). If questions from your young child about sexual organs, sexual function, and related topics have been sparse, honestly look at how available and open you have been. If a child feels you are uncomfortable with a topic, he or she will protect you by not asking about it.

Following are a variety of questions that you may be asked, along with some suggested replies that you should adapt to your needs. Never fear being too specific or giving too much information; do not underestimate your child's need and right to know.

Questions about Body Parts and Functions

What's this (pointing to the umbilicus)?
Your umbilicus. Sometimes we call it a belly button.

What's the umbilicus for?
Nothing now. Before you were born, you got all your food

and air through a tube that attached to your umbilicus and to Mommy. The tube is called the umbilical cord.

What's this (pointing to the penis)?
A penis.

Why don't I have one?
Because boys and girls are made differently. Boys have penises and girls have vulvas.

What's a penis for?
A boy uses his penis for urination. A girl's urine comes out of a different place, in the vulva.

What's a vulva for?
A vulva has several parts. There's an opening for urine to come out, a clitoris, and an opening to the vagina.

What's a vagina for?
It's a tube that goes from the special place a baby grows to the outside of the body. The baby goes through it to be born.

Why is my vagina dirty?
Your vulva and vagina are not dirty. But they are close to your anus where your bowel movements come out, so you must be careful that the germs in your bowel movements don't get near the vagina. That is why you always wipe from front to back and wash your hands carefully after going to the bathroom.

Can I stick my finger in my vagina?
If your hands are clean and you are gentle, yes. But never stick anything else in your vagina.

Can Tommy stick his finger in my vagina?
Our bodies belong to us. They are private. It's best if we not allow others to touch our private parts unless a doctor needs to examine us in his or her office or at the hospital.

What's this (pointing to the clitoris)?
Your clitoris. It feels good when you touch it, just like a
boy's penis feels good when he touches it. When you touch it
to feel good, make sure you are in a private place like the
bathroom or your bedroom with the door shut. People like it
better and feel more comfortable when they have privacy.
(For a more complete discussion of masturbation and the
young child, see Chapter 13.)

Why is my penis (Why are my breasts) so small?
It is just the right size for you. When you grow, your penis
(breasts) will grow too.

Why does my penis gets bigger when I rub it?
All penises do that; it feels good.

What's this (pointing to the scrotum)?
Your scrotum. It holds testicles, which feel like two balls.

What's a testicle for?
A testicle is the special place that makes sperm so a daddy
can help make a baby.

Why don't Scott and I have hair like you and Daddy do?
Children don't have hair around their penis or vulva but
you will when you grow up.

Why doesn't Daddy have big breasts?
Everybody has breasts, but grown-up women's breasts are
larger so that they can make milk and feed babies.

Can I touch your breasts (penis)?
No, children and adults should not touch each other's private parts. However, a doctor may need to look at your body to
see if you are well or sick. Also, we have to touch little babies'
private parts to keep them clean.

Why can't I sit down (stand up) to urinate?
You can; just make sure you clean up any spills.

Questions about Arousal and Intercourse

What is sex?
Sex is a nice grown-up way of being close.

Why is the door locked?
Mommies and daddies need private times all by themselves.

I want a private time with you.
Fine. It's important that people who care about each other be alone together sometimes.

Can I make love?
Mommy and Daddy believe only people who are married and grown-up should make love. When you are married and grown-up, you will make love.

Questions about Conception and Birth

Where did I come from?
You grew in a special place inside Mommy. All babies grow inside their mommies in a special place.

Did I grow from a seed?
No, flowers grow from seeds. An egg from the mommy and a sperm from the daddy start a baby growing in the special place.

What is this special place called?
The uterus. The mommy produces eggs in her ovaries, and the daddy makes sperm in his testicles. A sperm from the daddy and an egg from the mommy must join together before a baby can begin to grow in the uterus.

Why do you put pieces of paper between your legs, Mommy?
Mommy is having her period. Each month the uterus bleeds a little, and a bandage must be used. The period keeps the uterus healthy, but it doesn't hurt Mommy.

Does it hurt to have a baby?

A mommy's body is made so that she can have a baby, but it is a lot of work to push the baby out, and she can get very tired and sore.

When can I have a baby?

Mommy and Daddy believe that you shouldn't have a baby until you are married and know that you can take very good care of it.

Why can't boys have babies?

It takes a mommy and a daddy to have a baby, but the uterus happens to be in the mommy.

What does a baby eat when it is inside the mommy?

The mommy supplies the food through a tube, called the umbilical cord, that leads from her body to the baby. The end where the tube used to be is the baby's umbilicus or belly button.

How can the baby go to the bathroom before it is born?

Since a baby inside its mommy doesn't eat solid food like we do, any waste it produces leaves the body through the umbilical cord, the tube connecting the mommy and the baby.

7

The School-Age Child

The guys—all fourth and fifth graders—were spending the night at Darren's house. Somewhere between the pizza and the popcorn the conversation inevitably turned to sex. Joe, whose father was a doctor, held his buddies in rapt attention with the graphic details of how a father and a mother come together to make a baby.

Young Jonathan listened with amazement. "Yuk!" he snorted with disgust as Joe concluded. "That means my parents had to do it twice to get me and my sister!" (What a difference a few years will make in Jonathan's perspective!)

Before long the discussion drifted to the topic of who was sexy. Roger said their classmate Maggie was sexy. Darren's vote was for Stacy, and Lee agreed. Nominations ceased, however, when Greg suggested that Mrs. Garcia was sexy. "Mrs. Garcia? Shawn's mom?" Darren wanted to make sure he had heard right. Greg's nod was met with groans and laughter from his friends. Obviously Greg had missed something in Birds and Bees 101, they all thought.

"This is the way it is," Darren announced with self-imposed

authority, determined to set his friend straight. "Mothers can't be sexy."

I remember when my daughter, Malika, went through this stage. She was just beginning to comprehend the concepts of morality. She understood the sexual basics, but her interest in such matters had gone underground while other activities crowded in. Modesty, a greater need for privacy, and a bit of shyness changed Malika from an uninhibited baby to a typical, watchful school-age child.

One day, however, her inner ponderings bubbled to the surface. "I know all about sex," she told me, "but I don't know anything about 'the birds and bees' like my friends do. Would you tell me what I've been missing?" Malika was relieved and a little proud when she realized that she not only already knew about the birds and the bees, she also knew the proper terms.

The Facts and Nothing but the Facts

Contrary to appearances, school-age children (ages six to eleven) are still interested in learning about sex. Sometimes it seems that all our good teaching about sex and sexuality during our kids' preschool years is for naught. We think this way when we find them giggling at the nude statues in the museum or loudly and publicly ridiculing the personal sexual experimenting they are all still doing in private. But school-age children only appear to be disinterested in sex because the horizons of their world are wider, their exploration is reduced, and they are more adept at hiding their sexual interests.

Developmentally, these children are finally capable of putting their feelings into words instead of acting them all out. Grasping the idea that they don't need to act on every feeling has a positive, long-term effect on their sexual functioning. They learn how to choose their sexual responses instead of merely reacting to their sexual urges.

According to Erik Erickson's concept of child development, the chief task of the school-age child is mastering basic academic skills and content. The culmination of the stage occurs when the child emerges with a sense of competency derived from learning how to read, write, add, subtract, etc. Competency leads to a healthy self-image. A child who is competent knows what's going on. He is much less vulnerable to peer pressure and more capable of making responsible decisions.

Since the child's world is content-oriented, we can add a knowledge of sex to the list of skills he must acquire. This is not the time for discussing many personal specifics with him; he is far more comfortable with generalizations. But it is prime time for encouraging the development of sexual attitudes and the accumulation of facts.

The school-age child wants good answers. Foggy ones create more questions for him than solutions. He is too busy for lectures; he wants to skip right to the question-and-answer time. His questions are often complicated, but he doesn't expect us to know everything, just to be willing to listen and talk. When you provide accurate and reliable sexual information, discuss his questions openly, express your opinions and values clearly, and accept his individual needs, you provide your child's ticket to healthy sexual growth.

Monitoring Sex on the Media

During this stage of development children generally watch more TV and are exposed to more sophisticated programming. Parents must carefully monitor the input they receive from the media, particularly television. It is easy for the child to wrongly conclude from television that sex is always linked to violence, selling products, or cursory relationships. One study revealed, for example, that subjects with greater exposure to violent sexual materials tended to believe that women are responsible for preventing their own rape, that rapists should not be severely punished (they are normal), and that women should not resist a rape attack.[1]

It is futile to try to censor every objectionable scene or word from a child's TV menu. But you can strive to maintain a balance. Even the questionable material your child sees on TV can be used as a springboard for teaching. However, this means that you must be watching with him, not planting him in front of the TV while you are busy elsewhere.

I recently watched a portion of the Grammy music awards on TV. The obvious "in" thing for the celebrities was to cross-dress or appear as asexual as possible. I'm disturbed by such modeling because of its detrimental effect on our children. I'm not concerned that our kids won't know whether they are men or women (they've already figured that out by now), but rather that they will get a wrong perception of what it means to be a man or a woman.

A healthy child has a strong sense of who he is and how he fits in with the members of both sexes. This is not achieved by telling him that some tasks are only for men and others are only for women. Rather it is effected by the high esteem and proper attitudes we hold toward each sex. The Bible and the Judeo-Christian tradition unquestionably form the basis for proper sexual roles and attitudes. As in other areas of life, we must unabashedly define, model, and reinforce biblical roles and attitudes toward sex. We can hardly blame a child for adopting a confusing, asexual dress style or attitude if we fail to provide him with a healthy alternative.

There will be times when your values conflict with what your child is motivated by our society to think or do, and you will have to say "No!" Your child will survive strong prohibitions in areas of sexual attitudes and behavior if they are communicated in love, if you model the positive side without hypocrisy, and if his identity and sexuality are solidly founded. We are all too aware of the tragic results of strong prohibitions presented without love. Jesus had much to say to the Pharisees about that.

Always Bare the Truth

Have you ever wondered why we visit an art gallery and appreciate the nudes, but then go home and self-consciously undress in the closet in the dark? Somehow we have determined that our nude bodies are rather pitiful specimens in comparison to those in the gallery. We are embarrassed to see ourselves unclothed, let alone be seen in the buff by our spouse or our children.

Part of our problem with nudity is that we equate it with eroticism. This equation is not valid unless you deliberately intend it to be. Ask your local nudist if he finds running around a nudist camp erotic. He will quickly set you straight. It is concealment and secrecy that arouses interest and desire.

If your school-age child is going to grow up with a healthy attitude toward sex and sexuality, he must have a healthy attitude toward nudity. And remember: Your child will take his cue from you. If you run screaming into the closet when your child innocently walks in on you while you are undressed, or if you angrily bark at him for appearing in the family room without pants and underwear, you will convey a negative message about nudity. You are saying that the unclothed human body is something shameful, which also suggests that sex is shameful. However, an acceptance of nudity, both yours and your child's, implies that sex is a natural part of life like eating and sleeping. Most of us need to accept a certain amount of nudity as healthful and okay.

I'm not suggesting that you and your children become nudists, even in your own home. Sitting around the house nude is not relaxing for the majority of people, nor is it necessary to ensure a child's healthy sexual development. I'm simply saying that you need to become comfortable with nudity to the point that you are free from false shame and false modesty.

Nor am I suggesting that you eliminate all rules for modesty in your family. Change only those habits that have the potential to convey the wrong message—like always dressing behind locked doors or calling your child "naughty" if he chooses to dance through the house *au naturel*. Gradually alter your message by allowing your child brief glimpses of you in your underwear, leaving the door ajar as you change clothes, applauding your child's "nature dance" before you discuss with him its propriety, etc.

The one exception where strict privacy must be maintained is when you and your spouse are making love. A child doesn't need to know exactly what his parents do during their private times or how frequently they do it. As with the preschool child, if your school-age child accidentally walks in while you are making love, make sure you follow it up with a discussion.

Sometimes safeguarding against accidental viewing presents a problem, as on camping vacations when parents and children sleep in the same tent or recreational vehicle. Parents should determine beforehand how sex will be handled in these situations.

Dirty Words and Sexual Play

Little Alex announced to his mother, "Bobby is a 'dick'!" Reacting exactly as she should, his mother calmly asked if Alex knew what dick meant. Alex shook his head. She explained that dick was a slang word for a penis. To call someone by that name was derogatory. It was not a word that he needed in his vocabulary, since he knew the correct term.

Sometime later, Alex excitedly ran into the kitchen to proclaim the beginning of an exciting movie on TV: "Mom, come and see! Moby Penis is on!"

Alex learned that smart people know the correct words for body parts and functions. Most kids are like Alex; they respond very well to the explanation of slang words and just when and where they should be used, if at all. Just as you have been teaching the meaning of "private" when it comes to certain bodily functions, you must do the same with language.

Most families have words that are acceptable for use within the family, but are not used without. I remember being teased unmercifully by a friend who overheard us use the term "tinkle" with our children for urinate. A doctor's family, no less! How could we! We were thoroughly shamed until, the very next day, she asked her little girl if she needed to go "boom-boom"!

Sex play, at its height among four-year-olds, continues into school age. Sexual games encompass a wide variety of activities from "Doctor" and "Spin the Bottle" to group masturbatory challenges. Studies show that 39 percent of all 12-year-old boys have engaged in homosocial sex play, as have 14 percent of all nine-year-old girls. School-age sex games take on more of an elaborate mask with elements of chance (like "Spin the Bottle") and with courage and honor seemingly at stake (like "Truth or Dare" or "Consequences"). Such games are played by moral children who need an excuse to satisfy their sexual curiosity.

It is vital that we make our children aware that any game should grant equal power and be gratifying to all participants. Some damaged children can themselves cause great harm by devising games that are really vehicles for their anger or misuse of power. Applying psychological pressure through games such as "Chicken" or coercing compliance and secrecy is unhealthy. We must warn our kids against these activities. It has been proven that childhood sexual experiences that were abusive, forced, guilt-producing, harmful, or pressured affect adult functioning in the areas of family relations, contentment, marital satisfaction, and self-esteem.[2]

Try to view sex-play games from the perspective of the child. Children are motivated by a need to explore and learn about their world and to practice behaviors they have observed. They have no understanding of the meaning and significance adults place on intimate sharing.

You may be more comfortable steering your child away from sexual games. That's fine. Realize, however, that a great majority of people have participated in sex play with no repercussions.

Fighting the Cooties

Between the ages of five and 11 the sexes separate, although sexual interest is always secretly maintained. These are the years when carpooling takes 20 minutes longer because John won't sit next to Brandy for fear of contracting the dreaded disease of cooties. It's only after the mom-for-the-day threatens the dread disease of throttling that cooperation is achieved.

Both sexes are, in reality, consolidating their masculinity or femininity during this time. Children should already have a strong biological sense of their gender, so this time is spent learning how boys and girls and men and women behave—and exulting that you are a boy (or girl) because boys (or girls) are better.

Ryan, for example, was fascinated to learn at school one day that sex was determined by Y chromosomes and that it was the father who contributed the Y, thus determining the sex of his children. Ryan's usual after-school raid of the refrigerator that day was delayed long enough for him to go straight to the phone to call his dad (Dr. James Dobson) at the office. "Dad," Ryan shared, "thank you for making me a guy! Good-bye."

It is not unusual for school-age children to display stubbornly defiant sexist attitudes. These kids will mellow as they approach adolescence. If their sexist attitudes seem excessive, ask yourself what kind of model they are getting at home. Also explore the possibility that they are expressing these attitudes for their shock value. For example, a boy who must be Mr. Macho may actually suffer from insecurity about his masculinity.

Research on tomboys does not indicate that serious problems lie in store for such girls. (I am not referring here to children with serious gender confusion, but children who for a time explore exaggerated roles of cross-sex behavior.) They simply find that the competitiveness and greater physical activity of being "one of the guys" give them a healthy sense of competence and achievement. Most tomboys acquire more feminine traits and pursuits with the passage of time.

Within their respective groups, boys talk more openly and freely to their peers about sexual matters than girls. Girls, being generally less independent and more concerned with parental approval, talk far less about sex. Consequently they receive less information through the grapevine than boys.

However, anatomically and physiologically, many girls begin to outstrip their male counterparts as they approach the teenage years. I'll never forget as a young teacher measuring and weighing my seventh-grade class. A 205-pound girl topped the class, while the smallest member was a 64-pound boy.

Reassure children from age nine on that every person grows at his own special rate. Although girls begin to grow first, there are incredible variations between people, all within the confines of normality.

How to Bring "It" Up

The school-age child would rather clean his room than listen to a canned lecture on sexuality. The mere suggestion of such a talk will initiate groans and numerous protests along the lines of "Yuk! Gross! I already know all that." Instead, try opening up a discussion by saying something like, "When I was in school, we used to say the craziest things about sex (you might want to be even more specific). What kinds of things do kids talk about today?"

I'm a firm believer in holding discussions like these in front of the whole family—all ages, both sexes. The little ones will only process what makes sense to them, but they will learn that sex is an acceptable topic for discussion in the family. The older kids will learn that sex is something we can communicate about in mixed company. And everyone will learn that you are askable parents.

Your discovery of a *Playboy* magazine hidden in Tommy's bedroom can also serve as a launchpad for talking about sexuality. Instead of shaming him, point out the minimal amount of true love and caring expressed in these pictures or descriptions. Emphasize that it is the feeling of closeness that two people have that makes sex good, not what they do with their bodies. Admit that some people just consider the fun sex brings them, but that nothing is really fun if someone is being exploited. And in pornography, the female is almost always exploited.

If the thought of such discussions with your children frightens you, modify these suggestions within the confines of your comfort level. "What comfort level?" you ask. If you don't have one, pretend that you do. If all else fails, ask a trusted relative, friend, neighbor, or health professional to help you out. It's okay to explain to them that you were raised in a closed sexual environment and that talking about sex is difficult for you.

Questions School-age Children Ask

A school-age child typically has many questions about the growth and development of a baby. There is much concern expressed about the birth process itself, the health of the mother, and the potential for pain and complications.

Keep your answers general and simple. Be aware of the questions behind the questions!

Questions about Body Parts and Functions

Why does Jane shower with her family and we don't?
Every family sets rules that are best for them. Our rules may be different, but they work best for us.

Is it okay to undress in front of a friend?
If you are the same age and sex and the setting is appropriate, there is no harm in it. Our bodies are made by God, and we need not be ashamed of them. But it is always okay to be modest.

Why does Aunt Emma have large breasts?
Every woman has breasts that are just right for her. It doesn't matter how big or small a woman's breasts are, they are all able to produce milk for babies, which is why women have them.

What is puberty?
Puberty is the time in life when a kid's body changes to a grown-up's body.

Does puberty happen overnight?
No, it takes a number of years for a kid's body to change completely into a grown-up's body. Puberty begins and ends at different times for everyone. Usually it occurs between ages ten and 18.

Everybody in my class is starting puberty except me. What's wrong with me?
When puberty starts for you and how long it takes is just right for you. When you start has nothing to do with how big you will finally be.

When can a boy make a baby?

After he starts puberty and begins to produce sperm. That's usually between ages 12 and 16, but it varies with each boy.

When can a girl make a baby?

After she starts puberty and begins to release eggs. That's usually between ages 11 and 14, but it varies with each girl.

What's an erection?

When a man or boy has sexy thoughts or rubs his penis, extra blood flows into it, making it hard. When he stops thinking those thoughts or stops rubbing, the extra blood will leave and his penis will get soft again.

What's "the curse"?

"The curse" is a slang name for menstruation. We shouldn't use that name because it makes menstruation sound bad, even though menstruation really shows that a woman is healthy and that her body is working the way it should. Calling menstruation "a period" is all right.

Will it hurt when I start my period?

Sometimes women get cramps or backaches before and during their periods. These pains can be relieved by medicines or heating pads. Only a few women find they sometimes can't carry on as usual during their periods.

What are tampons for?

Tampons are like bandages. They fit in the vagina and catch the blood that flows during a woman's period. Tampons are changed regularly and can't be felt when they are placed properly. Some women use sanitary napkins, or pads, instead of or in addition to tampons. Pads fit inside the underpants to catch the flow of blood from the outside.

I'm the only girl in class who hasn't had a period. Why haven't I started?

Every girl grows at a rate that is just right for her. The range for starting periods covers a number of years. If it would make you feel better, we could make an appointment with the doctor for a checkup.

Questions about Arousal and Intercourse

What is "making out"?
Making out usually means that two people are kissing, hugging, and being very close.

Is making out wrong?
The Bible tells us not to get into situations where we can't control ourselves. Sometimes when people who aren't married make out, it feels so good that they lose control and want to have sex. All our actions with the opposite sex should glorify God. Sometimes it's hard to obey God when we allow ourselves to think only of how good something feels.

What does "horny" mean?
Horny is a slang expression that means someone feels like having sex or making love. Making love is a very pleasurable kind of sharing that grown-up people do.

How does a person know about making love when he gets married?
Sometimes people don't know very much about sex when they marry. They learn to be comfortable with each other and talk a lot about what each one needs. You can't expect to know everything when you marry, for each relationship is special for those two people. Reading books and asking questions helps, so the people at least know what generally happens and aren't afraid.

When do people usually start having sex?
Our bodies are able to have sex long before we should. Mommy and Daddy believe you should be married before you have sex, because that's one of God's rules.

Why did the lady on TV spend the night and make love with a man she wasn't married to?

Not everyone believes as we do about sex. Some feel it is okay for them to share their bodies without being married. God wants us to keep our bodies holy and be sexual under His rules. He promises that if we use our bodies as He intended, we will find the greatest satisfaction.

Is sex a sin?

God made us so that men and women would want to have sex in order to have children, feel especially close, and experience pleasure. But He also made rules that tell us how we are to be sexual. When we break His rules, we sin. But sex itself is a gift from God.

I heard fighting in your bedroom last night. Did Daddy hurt you?

No, Daddy and I were making love. Sometimes the noises of making love may sound like fighting, but they're not.

Do you make love every time you have a private time with Daddy?

No, sometimes we talk, joke, or read. We make love when we both feel very close and want to show how we feel.

What do you do when you make love?

The way people make love is private and special between the two of them. Often it involves a lot of touching, talking, and sharing. It can be lots of fun and make them laugh, or it can be very serious. Usually each time is just a little bit different.

Does making love hurt?

No, it shouldn't. It feels very good for most people, and they do it even when they aren't planning to make a baby.

How often do people make love?

That's personal and private between the two people. Usually people make love when they feel very close and want to show how they feel. It could be once a day or once a month. Whatever the two of them decide is okay.

What is a climax (orgasm)?

A climax (orgasm) is an especially good feeling that lasts for a fraction of a second to several seconds after a person's genitals have been touched and rubbed by intercourse or through self-pleasuring.

Does a climax (orgasm) feel the same for a man and a woman?

We don't know for sure, but from what people say, they are probably very similar.

How do boys/men and girls/women masturbate?

It varies with each person. Most of the time boys/men use their hands to stroke and rub their penis. Girls/women sometimes rub their thighs together or massage the vulva and clitoris with their hands. Sometimes they may gently place a finger into the vagina. Concerning masturbating, Mommy and Daddy believe (express your view on the appropriateness of masturbation). (Chapter 13 contains further information on this topic.)

Do men ever make love to other men, and do women ever make love to other women?

Yes, but when they do they are breaking God's rules for sex. God intends sex to be shared by a man and woman who are married to each other. We call men who have sex with men or women who have sex with women homosexual or gay. Sometimes female homosexuals are called lesbians.

What is an STD (VD)?

There are some diseases that can only be caught by having sex with a person who has the disease. We used to call them venereal diseases or VDs. Now we call them sexually transmitted diseases or STDs.

Questions about Conception and Birth

What are sperm?

Sperm are tiny cells with little tails produced by daddies in their testicles. When a mommy and daddy make love, the daddy releases millions of sperm into the mommy's vagina. The sperm move their little tails and swim through the vagina and uterus into the Fallopian tubes. If a tiny egg from the mommy is in one of the tubes, one of the sperm can join it and a baby is started.

How does the daddy's sperm get in the mommy?

When a daddy and mommy make love, the daddy places his penis inside the mommy's vagina to release his sperm.

How does a baby get to be a boy or girl?

Some of the sperm from the daddy are boy sperm and some are girl sperm. If a boy sperm joins the egg in the mommy, the baby will be a boy. If a girl sperm joins the egg, the baby will be a girl.

If the baby in the uterus is in a bag of water, why doesn't it drown?

A baby in the uterus doesn't breathe as we do. It gets its air from the mommy through the umbilical cord.

Can a mommy and daddy make love when a baby is inside the uterus?

Yes. A baby is protected inside the uterus.

Where does the baby come out?

When it's time for the baby to be born, it is pushed out of the uterus into the birth canal or vagina. It moves slowly down the birth canal and comes out the vaginal opening.

What is a Caesarean birth?

Babies are meant to leave the uterus through the vagina. Sometimes, because of special problems such as a baby being very big, the doctor must perform surgery, open up the uterus, and take the baby out. That's called a Caesarean birth. Because it involves surgery, the mommy usually has to spend a few extra days in the hospital. Babies delivered this way are just fine.

Why do mommies go to the hospital to have their babies?
Usually having a baby goes just the way it is supposed to. But in case there are problems such as the need for a Caesarean birth, mommies and daddies like to know that a doctor is nearby to help them.

Why is the lady down the street who isn't married having a baby?
Our bodies are capable of having babies whether we are married or not. Mommy and Daddy believe that God's plan for us to be married first is the best.

What are contraceptives (birth control)?
Contraceptives (or birth control) are methods to keep the daddy's sperm from joining the mommy's egg and making a baby. Mommies and daddies usually don't want to make a baby every time they make love, so they may use contraceptives such as pills taken orally or jellies or foams placed in the mommy's vagina. (Contraceptives are discussed more completely in Chapter 13.)

Can a dog and a person make a baby?
No, only people can make people, and only dogs can make dogs.

8

The Adolescent

Sixteen-year-old Chuck and his friend Brent had just finished a challenging game of one-on-one. "Hey Brent, I've got a question." Chuck was a brand new Christian, and Brent was the guy most reponsible for bringing Chuck to Christ. Chuck admired Brent and knew that he could depend on him for discerning advice.

"Shoot," Brent replied in his usual friendly manner.

"Now that I'm a Christian, how far can I go with a girl?"

Brent shot right back. "How far would you like someone to go with your future wife?"

Chuck's knees buckled slightly. "Wow!" he exclaimed. "I've never thought about it that way before." Chuck was hoping for an arbitrary boundary that he could push around if he didn't like where his clean-living buddy placed it. But this? Chuck was just beginning to understand what being a new person in Christ really meant!

How grand that God gives us teenagers to raise! Without them we might all rest on our laurels and gloat about our achievements at parenting toddlers and children. Instead, with adolescents in our home we are continually challenged to be more patient, more creative, more loving, and more humble than ever—especially when it comes to their sexual development and education.

Many of the young child's conclusions about life are based on how consistently and lovingly his physical needs are met. The adolescent is just as vulnerable. Many of his conclusions about life will be colored by how consistently and lovingly his *emotional* needs are met. For this reason I encourage moms and dads, if at all possible, to arrange work and/or volunteer schedules so that one of them can be home whenever their charged-up teens charge through the door. It is the one time that the normally taciturn teen will give some clue about the innermost working of his complex and often befuddling persona.

Who Am I?

According to Erik Erickson, the task of the young adolescent is to discover his identity. This involves developing skills that help him evaluate his career and sex role. Failure to accomplish this task results in role confusion. Success results in the affirmation of self and the ability to stand firm in what he believes.

Many young adults never successfully resolve this stage. They enter sexual liaisons before they have developed the cognitive decision-making skills they need to enable them to remain faithful in relationships. This negative learning, as they bounce from one love affair to another, colors their attitudes about future commitments.

It's appropriate that teens experiment with new behaviors. Each new fashion or hairstyle symbolically provides identification with a group or lifestyle our teens may decide to try on for size. How radical these endeavors are is determined by a combination of how effectively we have modeled being "in the world but not of it" and how much independence and self-worth our children possess. The influence of their peers in these experiments is of equal importance, so pray that they find friends like Brent.

Lest you fear that the "years of the gonads" will be inevitably difficult for you and your teen, child development experts assure that only a third of all teens have a really rough and rebellious time with adolescence. Another third have their moments, and the rest just wonder what all the fuss is about. Be encouraged; you have a 67-percent chance of getting through relatively unscathed!

These same experts say that we are more likely to encounter trouble with our teens if we try to maintain control by heavy-handed authoritarian tactics. Sometimes an over-controlled child must prove to himself or herself, "I am my own person." Such children need approval and acceptance from us, even if we have to close our eyes to the purple Mohawk hairdo in order to find something concrete and positive to say. We will face similar problems if we swing to the other extreme of control by opting for the laissez-faire approach. Balance works better.

Children No More

In order to help our children survive the identity crisis of their teen years, especially in the area of their sexuality, we must understand the radical changes which take place in their bodies. In just a few short years smooth-skinned little boys suddenly become muscular, hairy (at least in a couple of places) young men. Cherubic little girls are transformed into shapely young women. And their parents shake their heads and wonder what happened to their babies.

The Developing Young Man

Although they appear much less mature than their female peers, boys are only six months behind girls in their ability to reproduce. Their first ejaculation (remember: orgasms have been occurring since birth) will generally occur three to four months after the first downy pubic hair turns coarse and curly.

The majority of boys will go through a growth spurt between 12½ and 16, with major growth occurring around 14. Production of sperm varies, but it often begins about a year after the penis and testicles have started to grow, near the peak of the growth spurt. Changes in the voice and the growth of underarm hair will usually begin a few months after the first ejaculation.

Nocturnal emissions, or wet dreams, are the body's way of taking care of excess sperm. It is important that your teen boy know about them in advance and be assured that they are normal. Development of male breast tissue can also be upsetting if young men are not forewarned that it is a temporary and common occurrence.

Acne is more of a problem for boys than for girls, and it can be a source of great embarrassment. Good hygiene and diet may help reduce the problem for some, but the severity is usually more genetically related. Often parents can ease the pain by sharing their own experiences with acne.

The Developing Young Woman

In many cases girls begin adolescent growth a full two years before boys. Their spurt may begin at 10½ and be over by 14. Often menstruation will start about three-fourths of the way through, although ovulation can easily occur before their periods begin. Breast development begins three to four years before the onset of the period, pubic hair one and a half to two and a half years before, and underarm hair six months before.

When my mother was a child, my grandmother told her practically nothing about menstruation, allowing her to think she was being punished for something. As a result, my mother prepared me for menstruation, or at least she tried. By the fourth grade—none too soon for my body chemistry—I knew the facts; at least I knew as much as I could glean from the book she gave me on a subject I had never heard about before.

It sounded rather thrilling, a special happening reserved "for women only." My enthusiasm was quickly stifled by the embarrassed look and silence from the lady next door as I shared my juicy tidbit of knowledge with her. Humiliated, I retreated to my room, determined never again to commit such a faux pas.

Years later my young bridegroom nearly lost an arm when he inadvertently charged into the bathroom while I was changing a tampon. I slammed the door so quickly he remembers it to this day! The thought of him seeing me attend to something so "shameful" resulted in a total panic reaction.

I often puzzle over the fact that I became a sexual therapist, since the book from my mother was one of only two incidents I can remember when sexual information was shared in my home. Sometimes as I teach I am struck by the humor of such an unlikely candidate becoming a sex expert. Let me encourage you: If I can develop a comfort level for talking with people about sex and sexuality, you can develop a comfort level for talking with your spouse and children about sex.

By age 16 most girls have had at least one period, even though subsequent cycles may be irregular. The menstrual cycle can vary from 20 to 35 days and still be normal. The length of the period and the amount of blood leaving the body vary with the individual.

Today, with thinner pads and smaller tampons available, girls can be relatively comfortable during their periods. (The danger of toxic shock is almost completely eliminated by changing tampons every three to four hours and wearing pads at night.) There is no reason an adolescent girl cannot use a tampon, except in rare cases when the hymen is totally closed, a situation requiring a doctor's attention.

Periods can be affected by such factors as stress, diet, and exercise. It is not unusual for girls who train rigorously for sports to cease having their cycle. It returns as they reduce the amount of training.

PMS (premenstrual syndrome) has been the subject of a number of books and magazine articles. Many of the common menstrual symptoms are found in PMS, but true diagnosis can only be determined by careful record-keeping. Disorders start anywhere from midcycle to a few days before the period and cease when menstrual flow begins. To be termed PMS, symptoms must be severe enough to disrupt normal daily living. Treatment should focus on the specific disorder suffered, as evidenced by a woman's record-keeping. The currently popular and often expensive "shotgun" clinic approach to PMS should be strictly avoided.

Your developing young woman must learn to recognize and make allowances for her monthly menstrual symptoms. I know, for example, that my confidence level is down a week before my period. I make sure not to make long-range decisions at that time on what I can or cannot do. Most common menstrual symptoms can be helped by antiprostaglandins, heat, moderate exercise, no caffeine, increased vitamin B, plenty of rest, plenty of water, herbal diuretics, and a balanced diet.

Discussing periods, like all other sexual matters, can and should take place in front of both sexes. Boys as well as girls need an understanding of what happens and how a woman may be affected.

Coming of Age

When girls have ovulated and periods have begun, and when boys have begun producing sperm as signaled by ejaculation, they are physically capable of reproduction. This is the culmination of what we refer to as puberty.

Many cultures and some ethnic groups have rites of puberty that signify to society at large and the child that he or she has "come of age." Bar or bas mitzvahs are common in the Jewish community, for example. Most Americans, however, see puberty pass with no fanfare. Since the time of dependency for American youth is much longer than in the past, some of the significance of puberty is lost, so rites of passage diminish.

I think it's important that children who reach the plateau of puberty are specially recognized by their parents. It is truly a remarkable and significant event. Although puberty no longer signifies imminent marriage, it is the transition from childhood to adulthood. In our home we made a point of taking our son out to dinner at the restaurant of his choice—just Mom, Dad, and Joey. It was a good time to reinforce how special he was to us and to share a few dreams. With Malika, the plan was for Dad to send her roses, one for each year of her age.

Richard Durfield, a pastor, suggests that parents have a "key talk" with their early adolescent. Mothers take daughters and dads take sons out for a special dinner and "a private, personal and intimate time with the child to explain conception, the biblical view of marriage, and the sacredness of sexual purity." The talk concludes with the presentation of a "key" ring (the key to the child's heart and virginity) to symbolize a commitment to God. The ring becomes a powerful reminder to the child of God's presence and desire for the teen. My only concern is that the key talk is not the only time such teaching and sharing occur![1]

Helping Your Kids Survive Adolescence

The teenager's identity and sexuality cannot be separated. His search for his identity is also a search for sexuality. Her search for her sexuality is also a search for identity. Here are several tips which may help you help your teenager succeed in this critical task.

Stay in Touch

The transition from childhood to adolescence is marked by an almost universal phenomenon: parents withdrawing physical affection from their children. Even those of us who adored cuddling, roughhousing, or hugging our youngsters find ourselves hesitating to do so during their teen years. At the very period of their lives that our children feel least accepted by us, we "prove" it by pulling away from them physically.

I know what you're thinking: "Jason acts like I have cooties when I become physically affectionate. Besides, I don't want him to become gay from too much touching"; "Courtney's becoming a beautiful young lady. She'll think I'm a lecher for touching her." True, teens are sometimes embarrassed when we are mushy in front of their friends, so don't embarrass them intentionally. But touching does not make people gay nor must it be interpreted as always leading to sex. Touching makes people healthy. It implies acceptance and respect.

If you have stopped all physical contact with your teen, work your way back slowly and in natural ways: a hand on the shoulder, a hug on the way out the door, etc. Hang in there, and your "grown-up" baby will someday make your day by returning the favor!

Accentuate the Positive, Eliminate the Negative

Do you remember learning about "shaping" behavior in biology class? Do you remember trying it on the most boring teacher you had and discovering that your smiles and attentive mannerisms manipulated the unsuspecting soul into delivering the whole lecture just to you?

Teens are just as susceptible to attention and affirmation. Accept the fact that setting the tone for a positive relationship is more your responsibility than his. Smile and positively reinforce the things you like in him. Before long those behaviors will be exhibited with twice the frequency.

Never lose sight of the fact that although Steve is six feet two inches tall, he is not yet an adult. He has every right psychologically to be a kid one day and a grown-up the next, maybe even to be both on the same day. I noticed this with my own son, particularly at the end of one of his "romances." The breakup was quickly followed by an almost audible sigh of relief and reversion to games and TV shows that appealed to him at a much younger age.

Your goal should be to do all you can to bolster the adolescent's flagging self-concept. Don't forget: Teen bravado is often a cover for a poor sense of personal worth. Continue to be the strong influence you have always been. The teen years are not the years to throw in the parenting towel, but they do herald a call to modify our approach.

Keep Listening

Roberto has two reasons for avoiding his father. First, he is afraid Dad will misunderstand him. Second, he is afraid Dad will give him advice. Unfortunately, Roberto's father lives up to his son's expectations.

Our teenagers have difficulty verbalizing their problems to us because we often view their sharing as a request for our advice or solutions. Being able to express their concerns is their first step to developing a plan to solve them. They share with us to crystallize their ideas, not necessarily to have us fix their problems. When we think we are responsible for fixing their problems, our ability to listen carefully is blocked, which may cause them to avoid sharing with us again.

I remember vividly a day when 13-year-old Joey was acting particularly surly. His hateful tone of voice was just about to earn him a trip to his room when I managed to quit reacting long enough to take a more positive approach: "You really seem down today." Silence. "I'm guessing you have a few things on your mind." A few things! An hour later we had moved from a bad test grade to concerns about whom he would marry, nuclear war, and if anybody really liked him! I discovered that active listening was as important for me with Joey at 13 as it was when he was three.

Here are a few more simple rules for communicating:

Don't tell them when you can show them. Kids hate being lectured to, but they are open to being shown.

Be open about your own thoughts and feelings. Teens will state where they stand more freely if you communicate where you stand, even when there is a difference of opinion.

Share your past with them. All children love to hear stories from their parents' life experiences, especially the mistakes. This is particularly true if the stories reflect the same fears and insecurities the children are dealing with.

Ask questions which show your interest. Questions should imply respect for the child or be directed toward stimulating further discussion. Listen carefully to his replies to affirm him as a valuable person. Resist the urge to respond with sarcasm or continual teasing.

Help Them Learn to Think

No parent succeeds in teaching kids how to develop personal standards or to control themselves sexually by force, anger, or fear. These emotions only teach the child not to get caught. By contrast, teaching our kids to think leads to the development of a conscience, that is, a sense of responsibility and judgment.

But this doesn't always happen smoothly. Discipline is in order if we really care for our kids, but physical punishment is out of the question for teens. Good discipline should be clearly defined and help the child grasp the relationship between behavior and consequence. To this end, restrictions are not bad consequences for teens if the connection between acting responsibly and freedom is made.

Self-control comes from being able to think through a plan and carry it out. Teens need help in learning how to do this. Teach them to ask themselves, "What kind of outcome do I want? What kind of person do I want to be in this setting? What action will please Christ?"

Monitor Media Input

We know our kids are *in* the world, but we don't want them to be *of* the world. This is difficult when the world permeates the media which is so attractive to our kids. For example, there are many movies showing in theaters and on TV that simply are not acceptable for Christian kids. I hope you manage to steer clear of the worst ones. If your family is like mine, however, you have found yourself watching something that was far from what you expected. Our solution has been to forbid our children to see a movie unless we attend with them or preview it and approve it. Even if a bad movie slips through, however, you can use it as a teaching device.

With the advent of cable television, questionable programming of all kinds is piped right into our home—or at least our neighbor's home or our child's friend's home. Technological advances are making the job of keeping our children from exposure to the world an increasingly difficult task. We must teach them to discriminate between good and bad input themselves. We must give them the tools they need to make decisions without us. We also need to pray a lot!

What Every Parent
Should Know About Dating

Your teenage boy has been spending long hours on the telephone. His sudden devotion to cleanliness has left everyone else in the family to shower in cold water. He actually volunteered to wash the car. He is getting ready for his first date, but are you ready for your teenager to date?

Joey's first date resulted in us taking a quick trip to the store for a book on manners. I thought we had prepared him, but when he left his date in the car and bought only one ticket to the event, I knew there were still a few rough edges!

Dating Do's and Don'ts

Appropriate dating behavior should be discussed long before the fact. Our teens should understand the importance of not exploiting their dates. However, if our sons and daughters grow up aware of our convictions because we communicated well while they were still listening, major confrontations can be prevented.

Most of us parents agree on what we *don't* want our kids to do: usually what we did. I am truly amazed, however, at how often parents set their children up for failure. Sometimes our former mistakes color our thinking.

We also need to discuss an appropriate dating age with our children prefereably before dating is even an issue. There is a strong relationship between early dating (before 16) and premature sexual involvement. A common reaction among conscientious parents of adolescents is to be overly restrictive with dating. This sets up an area of confrontation in which no one wins. Our teens want and need to be independent, and dating is their first practical step in realizing independence. If they don't leave us they will never be able to cleave to a spouse as Genesis 2:24 instructs. And if we don't let them date, either they will never leave or they will leave on their own terms—and those are both sad alternatives. Work with them to set up their dating boundaries.

Perhaps some of you who were raised in the era when going

steady was the rage are perplexed about the tendency of today's youth to group date. Actually, it is a very wise practice. Today's teen knows that with the chance for privacy, the freedom to come and go as they please, and the media pressure to be sexual, being alone together is a setup for premature sexual bonding. They are consciously or subconsciously aware that they're not ready for a sexual relationship, so they protect themselves by dating in groups—and they have a great deal of fun in the process. It's a trend you can feel good about and encourage.

Avoid Wars over Sex

Don't make sex an area of hostile confrontation. Teens see sex as a powerful and perversely fun way to get back at Mom and Dad. If you've already begun the battle in this arena, don't despair. Keep your perspective. Keep the lines of communication open so rebellion isn't necessary. Rarely do adolescents truly disagree with the values they have grown up with, provided you have been open about where you stand and nonhypocritical in living it.

Another way we parents tend to make problems for ourselves is to set up self-fulfilling prophecies about our kids' sexual activities. We are so convinced that our kids will become sexual that we offer them birth control devices, make remarks about how they are "scoring," or beg them to confide in us. If you assume your teen is guilty, he will most likely make your assumption a fact.

Ask your teen what he thinks about certain conduct instead of asking him directly what he is doing. Share your stories and hold your ground. In *How to Really Love Your Teenager*, Ross Campbell suggests that we handle differences by affirming our trust in our kids but our distrust of certain situations they might be asked to handle.

Our adolescents, especially the boys, need all the help they can get in support of their decision not to be sexually intimate. That choice is a healthy one and has value, but teens who make it are not very vocal. Your teen may think he's the only one in his school who isn't sexually active. Until other kids go public for abstinence, you must be his primary support.

Our teens need a plan for their gift of sex. "Just say no" is not enough. Think of the hours spent deciding on the right college, getting a driver's license, or meeting the requirements for graduation. Shouldn't equal time be given to sex, which is profoundly significant and has far-reaching effects? Without a plan your child is vulnerable to sexual initiation in the backseat of a car, pregnancy, STDs, and other unplanned and often regretted experiences.

Help your son and daughter develop and verbalize a personal plan for saving their sexual gifts for marriage. Talk through the issue using questions like these:

- Are you going to use sex for recreation or as the glue for a lifetime commitment?
- What will the circumstances be for the onetime event of giving your body to someone for the first time?
- Will your decision about sex be announced publicly or kept a secret?

Don't expect responsible sexual decisions from your teens if they have not been taught how to make them and allowed to practice making them. Once they have verbalized a plan for saving sex until marriage, a quick comparison of their plan with the situations they face makes deciding what to do a workable reality. Just remember to exercise plenty of compassion. Even teenagers aren't completely grown up. They are just learning to be adults, and they are going to fail, so allow room for their failure.

When Is Love Really Love?

The romantic notion of one special man who sweeps a girl off her feet and satisfies her forever is a burdensome myth to project on kids. Teens will feel a great physical attraction for someone (perhaps several someones), but their head, not their emotions, will determine whether what they feel is love.

The Bible speaks of three kinds of love: eros (passionate feelings), phileo (sharing fun and dreams), and agape (selfless, unconditional love). True love, the kind that makes a marriage succeed, involves all three. Are you modeling these three types of love with your spouse? Are you helping your teen determine if he is focusing on only one type of love or developing a healthy balance of all three in his dating relationships? Teens must realize that only well-balanced love will survive the rigors of dating and married life.

Time for Sex Education

Gordon no longer wants to listen to Mom or Dad because their intelligence has been steadily dropping since he turned 13. Many parents of teens like Gordon think this is the worst time for them to continue his sex education. I won't allow you to use that as an excuse not to try. Believe me: You have a positive influence over your kids even when they act as if they know it all and you know nothing.

At 15 I thought I was well informed. I could tell you all kinds of things about sex. But I didn't know men got erections, and I didn't know exactly what intercourse was. A friend of mine shared how shocked and distraught she was upon realizing she had been penetrated while sitting on a boy's lap in the car. She knew all about sex; she just thought intercourse could only occur in bed.

Your teen may not be quite that naive, but all teens have misconceptions about sex and holes in their knowledge. A study at Johns Hopkins University revealed that 59 percent of teens didn't know when the risk of pregnancy was greatest and 90 percent didn't understand that STD symptoms often go away. If you aren't talking to your teen about sex, he's getting his information from his peers who are likely to be as ignorant as he.

If you think your child will not confide in you, or if you cannot share with her about sex, give her an option: "Alexia, I know you must have a few things on your mind. If you have time someday, you might want to talk to Mrs. Stone, Pastor Stone's wife. She mentioned that she would be happy to talk with you if you make an appointment. You can always speak to me, but I understand that someone from outside the family has a different perspective."

Indirect questions are a good technique for introducing discussions on sex, questions such as "What are the kids at school saying about all the news stories on sexual molestation of children?" Leaving good books about sex and sexuality lying around is another good method. But a parent who is available and askable, has a nonjudgmental attitude, and has a willing spirit is still the very best sex education method.

Questions Adolescents Ask

Even teens who have decided to save sex for marriage ask questions about sex. They don't ask because they want to experiment; they just want to know about it. They are in the stage of processing information that will be useful later. Don't be alarmed at what they ask. And don't give them the run-around on any topic. Remember: Whatever they don't learn from you they will learn from someone else, perhaps some-one with bad information.

The following questions are typical of those asked at this age level. Some teens are more inquistive about sexual mat-ters than others, however. Consider also the questions at the end of Chapter 9, because your teen may be ready to ask them as well.

Questions about Body Parts and Function

What can I do when I get an erection and don't want it?
Ignore it, think of other things, and it will go away. It is not uncommon for young men to be stimulated when emotions are high as when playing sports or dancing with a girl. As you get older, stimulation will tend to occur within more appro-priate settings.

Can wet dreams be controlled?
No, and there is no need to try to control them. Wet dreams, or nocturnal emissions, are a part of God's design for men. After puberty, sperm are constantly being produced in your testicles. If they are not released through intercourse or masturbation, they are released naturally and unconsciously while you sleep.

Can a boy ejaculate without touching his penis?
Yes. Sex has as much to do with the mind as with the body. It is quite possible for boys to have orgasms with mental stimulation only.

Can a girl have an orgasm without stimulating her clitoris?
Yes, through mental stimulation and through stimulation of different parts of the body that are particularly sensual to her. Some women find the lower third of the vagina, or a sensitive spot sometimes called the G spot within the vagina, particularly arousing.

Do women ejaculate?
This is debated, but probably not. However, some women report a rather profuse release of fluid from the urethral opening which seems to be similar to an ejaculation.

What is a virgin?
A virgin is a man or a woman who has never had sexual intercourse. There is really no sure physical way of telling a virgin. It seems though, that Christians need to avoid the hypocrisy of claiming physical virginity while having done everything sexually except intercourse.

Can a girl use tampons while she is a virgin?
Since the hymen rarely seals off the vaginal opening completely, most girls can use tampons.

How long does a period last?
Usually anywhere from three to seven days. Each girl's body will establish its own pattern, and that will be right for her.

Is masturbation wrong?
The Bible does not speak for or against masturbation, and opinions among Christians vary. As your parents, we feel _____. However, if your lustful fantasies become more important to you than your walk with God, it is clearly wrong. (See Chapter 13.)

What is a "queer"?

Words like "queer" or "fag" are derogatory and offensive slang terms for a homosexual. Using terms like these violates a number of biblical passages, such as Ephesians 4:29: "Do not let any unwholesome talk come out of your mouths, but only what is helpful for building others up according to their needs." People who are sexually attracted to the same sex are called homosexual or gay. Sometimes female homosexuals are called lesbians. Homosexuality is clearly against God's plan. (See Chapter 13 for further discussion of homosexuality.)

Can you identify a homosexual by his appearance?

No, not all homosexuals act in ways that indicate they are gay. Most of the time you would not know.

Why do some people want to change their sex?

No one knows for sure. Some people sincerely feel they were meant to be the opposite sex and are "trapped in the wrong body." Some may suffer from hormonal problems. Sex-change surgery is rarely done today.

What is a transvestite?

A transvestite is a person who likes to dress in clothes of the opposite sex. Most are married men who are not homosexual. Many have had early childhood experiences that reinforce a desire to cross-dress.

What is a transsexual?

A transsexual, unlike a transvestite, truly feels he or she is supposed to be the other sex. A male transsexual doesn't see his attraction to men as homosexual, because he considers himself to be a woman.

Do alcohol and marijuana affect sex?

Yes. Alcohol lowers your inhibitions, making it more difficult for you to resist sexual temptation. Increased consumption of alcohol reduces sexual drive and performance. Marijuana reduces the amount of testosterone production, affecting fertility and drive for long-term users. Marijuana may artificially heighten the sexual experience for occasional users, but what good is artificial sex?

Questions About Arousal and Intercourse

Men get an erection when they are aroused. What is the counterpart in women?
Women release a lubricant through the walls of the vagina.

Sometimes I think about someone who is attractive to me in ways that I shouldn't. Am I evil?
You can't prevent sexual thoughts from passing through your mind. But if you hold onto them, add to them, or elaborate on them in your imagination, you only increase your desire to act them out. Acknowledge your thoughts, then turn your focus to more appropriate aspects of the relationship.

Why should I wait until marriage to have sex?
Most important, it's God's plan that you reserve sex for marriage. However, there are many other good reasons for waiting. Here are several to consider:

- Although you're physically grown up, your convictions on what is right and wrong are still developing. You may choose to be sexual for the wrong reason, such as rebelling against your parents or thinking you won't be loved or popular if you aren't sexually active. Your teen years are filled with searching and confusion, and this is not the best time to make decisions with such long-lasting consequences.
- If you become sexually involved with someone, you will spend so much time together that you will exclude other friends and experiences you need to grow emotionally and socially.
- You will likely be physically attracted to many people before you find the person who meets your needs as a

lifelong partner. Most couples decide to be sexual because they plan to marry each other eventually. But marriage occurs only in 50 percent of those relationships. Only one out of five pregnant teen girls marries the father of her baby.

- The possibility of disease is another reason for waiting. The younger a person starts to have sex, the more partners he or she will have. Four partners increase a girl's chance of getting Pelvic Inflammatory Disease (PID) threefold. PID can cause pain, bleeding, and infertility problems. If the girl is a virgin and the boy has had four previous partners, he increases her chance of developing cervical cancer by as much as 10 percent.

- Promiscuity in the teen years can result in relationship problems later in marriage. Sexual counselors know that memories of past relationships can negatively affect current relationships. It is hard not to compare or fantasize about previous experiences.

How can I say no when I feel like saying yes?

Sexual feelings are very powerful. When you think they are bigger than you, remember that God is bigger still. Knowing your value system and deciding what you want and don't want *before* you are pressured by those feelings is a great help. Developing a plan in the heat of passion doesn't work. It is also smart to stay out of situations that cause those feelings to well up. Check out a book on creative dating, and date in groups.

How can I know if my boyfriend really cares about me or if he is just using me?

Consideration for your needs, feelings, and value system is a good test. A person who asks for "proof" of your love is in love with himself and his own needs.

How far can I go sexually?

You should be able to decide by answering these questions: How far would I like someone to go with my future wife or husband? How does what I'm doing express my commitment to God and His Word? How am I building up my partner's idea of himself or herself? Will my actions glorify the Lord?

My boyfriend tells me that everyone is doing it. How should I respond?

Tell him that you're not everyone—you're someone special (you are!). Get your friends together and come up with your own special comeback lines!

My girlfriend says I don't really love her if I don't have sex with her.

If she really loved you, she wouldn't ask you to do something you're not ready for or that is against your religious beliefs. Sex is never proof of love.

If I've already been sexually involved with someone, why stop now?

It makes a difference to God. He cares what you do from this moment on. Not becoming involved again or stopping involvement is difficult. It requires more than good intentions. You need to examine your lifestyle and change your habits. God honors a person who desires to live righteously, and He provides strength to help you do what seems impossible to do on your own.

Questions About Conception and Contraception

When is a girl most likely to get pregnant?

When she ovulates, which is midcycle—halfway between two periods. However, young girls have irregular cycles, so the timing is more difficult to figure.

Can a girl get pregnant if she doesn't have an orgasm?

Yes. Intercourse with or without orgasm can result in pregnancy.

Can a girl get pregnant if she is on top of the boy during intercourse?

Yes. Position has nothing to do with it.

Can sperm go through clothing?

There are millions of sperm in each ejaculate, and girls have become pregnant even though they have left on items of clothing. Clothes were not meant to be used for birth control.

If I skip a period am I pregnant?

You can only be pregnant if you have had intercourse. Many women miss periods because of stress, change of diet, exercise, travel, or other factors.

What happens when a person gets a sexually transmitted disease (STD)?

It depends on the disease, but symptoms often involve sores on the genitals and/or a genital discharge. By contrast, 90 percent of the women who have gonorrhea never know they have it. Advanced syphilis can lead to insanity. Herpes and AIDS have no cure. Both can be transmitted to babies by infected mothers and result in death. There is a new treatment for recurring herpes symptoms that helps some people have fewer and less severe reactions. Chlamydia is the number one STD among teens. It can cause Pelvic Inflammatory Disease (PID) resulting in pain, bleeding, and infertility.

Teenagers don't have to worry about AIDS unless they are homosexuals, right?

Wrong! Teenagers are at high risk because so many have unprotected sex. The STD rate is also high in teens which increases the chance of getting the AIDS virus. Drug use involving shared needles is another way teens increase their risk. Many people who now have AIDs contracted it as teens.

Are men more likely to get AIDS than women?

Actually, if a woman is exposed to the virus she is at increased risk. The disease progresses faster and women die sooner than men.

9

The Young Single

Dear Son:

Tomorrow you are on your own. Your mom and I pray that our job of rearing you has been well done and that you are prepared to meet the challenges you will surely face as you strive to be *in* the world but not *of* the world.

We know you love the Lord. We trust that you will remember that He is always with you in ways we never can be. We have worked hard to help you develop a good self-image and accept the sexual person God has made you to be. It is a source of great satisfaction to us that you respect and honor your body by treating it as the dwelling place of the Holy Spirit.

Our society says that you have come of age, implying that you are ready to marry and have a home of your own. Marriage is designed by God to be honorable and holy. If you are uncomfortable being single, we hope you'll trust the Lord's will and timing to bring you the woman who will enable your marriage to be what it was meant to be.

Please remember, Son: God mandated that we seek His kingdom first, not marriage (Matthew 6:33). A committed few have changed the world, and it is no accident that many were single. John the Baptist, Jesus, the apostle Paul, and many single missionaries over the years are responsible for the spreading of the Word to the ends of the earth.

Married or single, you are God's person. He will see that you become exactly what He wants you to be. Your job is to seek His will and learn to be content (Philippians 4:11). We are proud that you are God's person!

In His love,
Dad and Mom

Sigh! Wouldn't it be lovely to write such a letter to your soon-to-fly-the-nest "baby"—and mean it? Intellectually we know that equipping our children for being single or married is the right philosophy. But emotionally most of us are still convinced that real maturity comes with marriage. If our children are not married within a certain time limit, we begin to panic. We may even muse on where we went wrong!

Marriage is such a favored state that while one out of every two marriages fail, 80 percent of those who divorce remarry within three years. The number one excuse for first-marriage failure is "We were too young and too immature to make it last." But statistics prove that things get worse instead of better for later attempts. Seventy-five percent of all second marriages and 85 percent of all third marriages fail.[1]

It's Okay to Be Single

Singleness has an image problem. Singles are suspected of being gay, unable to relate, immature, or selfish. TV ads may portray the single life as glamorous and carefree, but the day-to-day image of singles is one of basic irresponsibility.

Even in our churches we belittle single status by emphasizing family picnics, couples' Bible studies, and activities within our homes. Rarely do we ask singles to fill important church positions. This subtle discrimination is part of an unconscious ideology so ingrained that we don't even recognize it as a biased view.

There are currently more singles in America than at any other time in our history. Soon 50 percent of our population over 18 will be unmarried. If you assume that statistic is due mainly to divorce, you are wrong. Forty-one percent of all people who are currently single have never been married.[2]

Why is marriage a less appealing alternative for so many? For some it's the attraction to greater economic freedom. Others are scarred from growing up in a divorced family or burned-out on intimate relationships from a series of failed love affairs. And there are a myriad of other reasons. Perhaps the tragic reality of AIDS and other STDs will slow down the trend toward singleness.

The sex education of our children must include the fact that there is nothing wrong with being single. It is irresponsible of us to push them toward marriage and family without acknowledging that God may allow them to remain single for many years or for a lifetime. The goal of our tutelage must be to release young adults into the world who are comfortable being married or single and who understand God's Word for either setting.

Singles Are Sexual Too

Despite what *Playboy* or Madison Avenue would have us believe, sex and sexuality originated with God. He designed us to be sexual creatures. Curiously, however, He left out of His design a switch by which we could turn our sexual feelings on or off depending on our marital status. Such a switch might have simplified matters for the Christian single. Clearly God expects singles and marrieds alike to accept their sexuality and express it within the Scriptural boundaries for their marriedness or singleness. God obviously believes that it's possible to be single *and* sexual. This perspective contradicts the secular message that a person will go crazy if he disciplines his sexual desires instead of acts on them.

Assure your single adult children that they have all the resources they need to function within the framework of God's design and plan for them. Remind them of Philippians 2:13: "It is God who works in you to will and to act according to his good purpose." Jesus is the truth and the way. They don't need to seek gratification for their sexuality in the singles' bar, Transcendental Meditation groups, or the health club (even though it's a healthier approach than some). The shallowness of these methods for finding purpose is obvious as we see one popular panacea abandoned overnight for a new one. The Bible helps us discern God's plan for singles from man's plan. We learn that singleness can be a spiritual gift enabling some individuals, unencumbered by family obligations, to spend more time and energy serving God (Matthew 19:10-12; 1 Corinthians 7:7,32-35).

Handling the Desire for Physical Love

Your son or daughter must learn that it is wrong to marry simply for the sake of being married. He or she must also learn that being single does not lead to asexuality but incurs a new plan for dealing with his or her sexuality. This plan involves accepting the sexual person he or she is. To deny sexuality is to deny a part of his or her personhood and, in that sense, deny the Lord who made him or her. Every time your son or daughter interacts with another person, he or she acknowledges his maleness or her femaleness.

But young singles are not switched-off sexually. They have the same level of desire for the physical expression of their sexuality as their married peers. How are they supposed to handle it? The Bible is unequivocal on the subject: The fullest expression of our sexuality is reserved for marriage. In light of this clear guideline, singles have several choices.

"Me? A Sexual Drive? Never!"

First, singles can repress their drive by pushing it out of their conscious mind and denying that it exists. There are several problems with repression, however. Those who try to turn off valid sexual feelings may find, to their surprise, that these feelings are turned back on with a rush at a most vulnerable time. Not having faced the strong emotions of the situation, they are easily overwhelmed and their bodies take control. And letting the body rule is prohibited in the Bible.

Nowhere does the Bible ask us to deny that we are sexual beings. We are, however, admonished to flee sexual immorality (1 Corinthians 6:18). Denial of sexual feelings, coupled with an "it can't happen to me" attitude, is probably behind the moral failure of many of our fallen spiritual leaders.

Young singles who depend on denial of sexual feelings to keep them in line are misunderstanding an important truth: It's not their feelings that are the problem; it's what they do with their feelings that sometimes gets them into trouble. We are feeling, responsive people by nature. To deny this is to deny the way God made us. Instead, singles must be fully aware that certain people, situations, and events can provoke in them a hungering for physical release. They must learn to acknowledge these feelings honestly and make themselves accountable to a trusted friend or pastor for how they respond.

Repression can also result in a person losing the ability to recognize and respond to natural sexual feelings when the setting *is* appropriate. More than once I have been called upon to counsel a young couple whose commitment to premarital sexual purity was right and honorable, but whose method of denial undermined the sexual relationship in marriage they had tried to protect!

"My Sexual Drive? I've Been Too Busy to Think About It"

Less powerful forms of sexual repression are suppression and its close cousin, sublimation. Some singles consciously or unconsciously redirect their sexual energy into work, creative pursuits, study, and sports. You've had the experience of going out shopping and getting so hungry you thought you would surely die. Then you ran into a long-lost friend and spent an hour rehashing old times—completely forgetting how hungry you were. Your stomach, which had been screaming at you to fill a very legitimate need, simply closed up shop when your attention was diverted elsewhere.

Similarly, when a young single fills his mind with other thoughts and his hours with other activities, he can quiet his very legitimate sexual drive. That's sublimation. Suppression and sublimation are probably the most widely practiced means of controlling the sex drive. There's nothing unhealthy about this process, but it's not 100-percent effective.

Distractions are especially helpful to young singles when they are enjoyed with a network of Christian friends who provide mutual support, caring, depth of relationship, and accountability. Our young adult children must be taught that platonic relationships can be a rich source of encouragement and diversion from their sexual drive.

These friendships will work only if the issue of sex is firmly and honestly faced. For a single to disclaim that sexual feelings exist, even between the most unlikely of his opposite-sex friends, is to risk being caught unaware. If he fails to face his feelings, he denies himself the opportunity to make insightful and healthy decisions for handling them.

It is highly unusual for a single adult to stumble into a sticky moral situation by accident. Rather, he slips morally because he has consciously or unconsciously decided on a series of supposedly harmless compromises with his sexual feelings. Here again accountability to others is good protection. We are called to bear one another's burdens. The single's quest to maintain moral integrity is indeed a burden in a society that does not respect moral absolutes or sexual self-discipline.

There are some young singles who, despite sincerely putting all of the above suggestions into practice, still find that their sex drives threaten to send them to the showers—at least three times a day. For those who are comfortable with it, masturbation is an option. Contrary to the myths, masturbation can be a tension reliever and a comfort for Christian singles if it is practiced with an attitude of thankfulness for a body capable of feeling pleasure and a focus on the physical release instead of a sexual fantasy. Secret sexual fantasies make life more difficult for the individual trying to exhibit self-restraint. Moreover, it is strongly spoken against by Jesus in Matthew 5:28: "I tell you that anyone who looks at a woman lustfully has already committed adultery with her in his heart."

A Disciplined Attitude

Whatever approach works most successfully for our single daughters and sons, sexual purity won't be a piece of cake. Even marriage isn't an easy answer in a society where women considerably outnumber men.

An active sex drive is not the only reason an individual may struggle excessively with sex. A number of other possibilities must be examined. What needs are being filled by sex that might be filled in other ways? Is loneliness the real problem? Does a low sense of self-worth make a single unable to say no? Is there a spirit of defeat which resigns, "Why bother? I've already been sexually involved." Is sex a means of power for this individual? Did early sexual experiences teach him or her that this is the only way to relate to the opposite sex? Is the motivation for sex a rebellion against parents, church, or God? Have habit patterns resulted in addictive behaviors?

Sometimes an honest evaluation of an individual's lifestyle is called for. What books, movies, or videos occupy his time and his mind? Whatever fills the mind will eventually be expressed in behavior. The proper mind-set is essential to sexual discipline. If an individual sees his body as the dwelling place of the Holy Spirit, we assume he would be careful about what he does with it or exposes it to. Yet it is rare for a Christian single to have both a healthy outlook about being single and the ability to resist the impulse to be sexually involved.

The majority of your young adult friends try to straddle the fence. Herculean effort is required for them to reject much of the popular music of the day, many of the movies, and most of the suggestive clothing, especially if their parents have been silent about moral values or stridently wailed about the decadence of the day without backing their stand with a biblical rationale.

No stretch of Bible interpretation can justify other outlets for the single's sexual drive, such as sex with other singles, adultery, or homosexuality. God promises that when we accept Christ the old ways are gone and we become new creations (2 Corinthians 5:17). Singles must never forget that their major resource will always be the Lord. God will be with them to help them live with themselves and move them toward being the people He wants them to be.

It is not unusual for an individual to be motivated to an illicit affair by his or her search for "okay-ness." We must help our young singles realize that there are far better ways to develop a sense of self-worth than through the vicissitudes of a love affair in which a partner's motivation for involvement can be quite neurotic. Are you teaching by contrast that the person who knows the will of God in regard to the use of his body and has set his course to follow that will is the real "catch of the year"?

A young adult's ability to think, determine, and manage his sex life with assurance and sound moral judgment comes from years of encouragement at home to stand up for personal beliefs. If a child learns that his value resides in being God's person, he is less concerned about being the person of Tom, Dick, or Mary.

This individual has self-discipline. If he is able to decide against sex before marriage, he likely has developed the self-discipline to resist illicit sex after marriage. Self-discipline also spawns a willingness to work out other life problems, for patience and persistence are a part of discipline. Maturity, a strong value system, and the ability to set aside ego needs and immediate desires to pursue long-term goals all indicate an individual who is able to make an unassailable marital commitment. By emphasizing these traits as highly desirable, you are maximizing your child's future marital stability.

When Young Singles Fail Morally

The physical ramifications of sex outside God's design are hard to live with, but the real challenge comes as the single struggles with the psychological and spiritual impact of moral failure. Guilt results in alienation from God as the individual avoids God by shunning prayer time and church attendance. Sin separates us from God, and being separated from God is painful.

Moreover, an act of illicit sex opens another Pandora's box when the young single wonders how many other people his partner has been with, how he measures up to other lovers, and how many others there will be. "Was she seeking the love of her life, or was she merely trying to find herself at my expense?" Seeds of distrust quickly sprout in such fertile ground.

God Forgives Sexual Sins

In Galatians 5:19-21 and Colossians 3:5-9 sexual sins are listed alongside a number of other condemned acts. Isn't it interesting that many Christians tend to isolate sexual sins from other sins as somehow being considerably more grave? In doing so we have unwittingly perpetrated the myth that God stands ready to forgive sins like anger, slander, and greed, but He's hesitant when it comes to forgiving sexual sins.

There are two reasons for the popularity of this myth. First, since all of us are guilty of anger and greed at times, we are only too happy to take the heat off them by focusing on a "worse" sin we can avoid or at least keep hidden. Second, 1 Corinthians 6:18,19 points out that sexual immorality is specifically warned against because it is the only sin man commits against his own body, the dwelling place of the Holy Spirit. Since sexual sins are distinguished in this way, we have deemed them less forgivable and sometimes even unforgivable.

The truth of the matter is that God is a patient and forgiving God, even when it comes to forgiving sexual sins. Aren't you glad and thankful for that, especially if you or your children have experienced moral failure? John 8:1-11 tells of the adulterous woman who was brought before the Lord. Caught in the very act, she didn't have the merest defense according to

Mosaic law. The penalty was stoning—no nebulous, legalistic double-talk here! But Jesus refused to condemn her and told her to go and sin no more.

Luke 7:36-50 records that the Lord's feet were washed by a prostitute. The men around Him were horrified, for by law merely being touched by a woman could render you spiritually unclean, and being touched by a prostitute required a purification offering. But Jesus had forgiven her, and He treated her as if she had never fallen. The prostitute's forgiveness resulted from the faith and love she expressed, not from her good works.

Forgiveness of sexual sin is preceded by confession. King David acknowledged and confessed his sin, asked to be washed clean, and accepted that he was a forgiven man (Psalm 32:1-5; 51:1-12). Acknowledging shortcomings and failures seems easy for most people, but accepting forgiveness is a concept that must be taught and demonstrated. If the Lord can forgive and forget David's confessed sins—and David was guilty of adultery and murder—He can certainly forgive and forget our confessed sexual sins and those of our children.

Some parents may object, "Our children will go wild sexually if they know their slate can be washed clean!" Perhaps, but only if we fail to instill within them the concept of a personal God with whom they have a day-by-day relationship. Jesus said, "If anyone loves me, he will obey my teaching" (John 14:23). Our children need to know that their relationship with God calls for loving obedience.

Also, our children may be sexually irresponsible if our discipline has ignored the natural consequences of their actions. They need to understand the long-term physical, psychological, and emotional repercussions of sexual sin. David's kingdom was affected for the rest of his days by the natural consequences of his immorality.

Even after a young adult has made a mess out of his life through sexual sin, if he truly loves the Lord and wants to walk in His way, Romans 8:28 promises that God will bring good out of the ashes of his life. I love author Harold Ivan Smith's reference to this process. He uses the analogy of a beautiful stained-glass window which is created out of broken pieces of glass. God can pick up the pieces of our children's broken lives and create a masterpiece.

Preparing Your Young Single
for Marriage

We have spent a lot of time talking about the importance of helping our young adult become comfortable living as a single. They also need to know that marriage is honorable for those who choose it.

Most of what your child has learned about marriage has come through osmosis—observing you and your spouse. Is this a scary thought? No marriage is perfect. But your adult children will have worse problems in their marriages if you cover up your problems and portray a front of perfection. Don't cripple your child's future marriage by pretending an angry word never passes between you and your spouse. Don't suggest that your adjustment to marriage was a breeze because you "really loved each other and the Lord." Give hope by painting a realistic picture that a good marriage is something that requires hard work. And working hard is something we choose and commit to do.

Why not plan to give your young single and his or her intended an engaged couples' weekend seminar. (Many local churches offer premarital conference programs, and some national marriage seminars are available.) There in a neutral setting they can evaluate their marital expectations and commitment.

God's ideal for marriage is hard to achieve in a fallen world. But that's what we shoot for. And our efforts do not stop with our own marriages. We are called to be the best mentors and encouragers we can to our starry-eyed young adults who are already planning a honeymoon at Disneyland!

Questions Young Singles Ask

Whether your young adult is planning to remain single or preparing for marriage, many of the following questions may come up if they have not been discussed during adolescence. The answers I suggest here are ones I have given to countless numbers of singles in my teaching and counseling.

Questions about Body Parts and Function

Can a man's penis be too big or too small for a woman's vagina?

A vagina is a collapsed tube that can expand to accommodate the passage of a baby. Its size is greater than any penis.

How big does a penis get during intercourse?

Most penises will reach about six inches in a fully erect state. When a penis is erect, there is very little difference in size from one man to another. But penis size is not what makes sex good. A good sexual relationship depends on how a husband and wife feel about each other and how well they communicate their needs.

Can anything stop the production of sperm?

Production of sperm can be reduced by certain illness, taking certain drugs, wearing tight underwear, or being exposed to extremes of temperature.

Can a woman have intercourse during her period?

There is no health reason for not having intercourse during a period. Often a couple choose not to because of the inconvenience.

What is menopause?

Menopause is the opposite of puberty for a woman. In puberty she begins to release eggs for fertilization. In menopause the woman ceases egg production.

Do men have menopause?

Physiologically, no. Some people feel that men experience the psychological effects of menopause even though they continue to produce sperm throughout their lives. We tend to call these effects a midlife crisis in men.

Questions about Arousal and Intercourse

Does a woman always bleed the first time she has sex?

No. Blood comes from a ruptured hymen. Often the hymen has been broken or stretched by the use of tampons or through vigorous physical activity such as sports.

Does intercourse hurt the first time?

Not always. But the majority of people don't find their first experience very pleasurable. Fear makes the body tense; sexual pleasure only occurs if the body is relaxed.

How does intercourse feel?

A satisfying sexual experience has a lot to do with what is going on psychologically. If a person feels right about the relationship and setting, then physically he or she will experience extremely pleasant bodily sensations that tend to increase in intensity. The physical sensations are actually caused by two things: blood flowing into the pelvic area and muscle contractions. Physical sensations can reach a peak, which is called a climax or an orgasm, after which a feeling of peace and relaxation occurs.

How long does intercourse last?

As long as both people are enjoying it and their bodies are not too tired.

Do older people make love?

Yes, many older people continue to make love no matter how long they live.

What is oral sex?

Making love usually involves a lot of different ways of being close. Kissing all parts of the body, including the genitals, is something many people enjoy. When a man kisses a woman's genitals, we call it cunnilingus; when a woman kisses a man's penis, we call it fellatio. You may have heard many slang words for oral sex such as "blow job," "69," "going down," or "giving head." None of these terms is very pleasant or polite to use.

What is sodomy?
Sodomy refers to anal intercourse. It is a sexual practice often associated with homosexuals, although it is also practiced by some heterosexuals.

Is orgasm during masturbation and intercourse the same?
No. Orgasm with masturbation is more intense. Most people prefer orgasm with intercourse because it involves interaction with another person, and that's more satisfying. Good sex involves more than just going through the motions physically.

How do homosexuals make love?
They do lots of touching, kissing, and holding like heterosexual couples do. But since they can't experience normal vaginal intercourse, there is more mutual masturbation and oral and anal intercourse. But remember: Homosexuality is clearly against God's plan.

Do men and women always disagree about sex?
Some men mistakenly think the only way they can be close to a woman is by being sexual. Cuddling, holding, and sharing feelings are not considered "macho" enough. Women seem to understand that intimacy is really what makes us feel loved and cherished, and that it can be established in many ways in addition to sex. Most differences can be compensated for by good communication.

I've already been sexually intimate with someone I thought I was going to marry. After we broke up I tried sex with someone else trying to get her out of my system. All it got me was more guilt and misery. What am I supposed to do?
Only half of all people who decide to have sex because they are going to get married end up marrying. As you have discovered, using sex in a way God didn't intend packs a powerful emotional punch. You can't pretend it didn't happen!
Before you can think of another relationship, you must unhook yourself from the original bond you established. Take

time to mourn the relationship that ended, the aspects that didn't come to fruition, and your failure to live up to God's standards for your sexual life. Cry and be sad. Confess your sin. Ask the Lord to help you.

The mourning process is very individualistic. It may require two weeks or two years. You will never completely forget what happened, but you will be able to place it into proper perspective in your life. As a Christian you can be a new person in Christ. I suggest you read Donald Joy's books *Bonding* and *Rebonding*.

I had my first sexual experience as a teenager. I decided I wasn't going to get sexually involved again since it is against my values. But each serious relationship seems to get to the sexual part faster than the last. What can I do?

Usually the first sexual experience is the result of a slow-blooming romance that the individual is convinced is true love. But with each new romance, the preliminary steps to physical intimacy are taken more quickly and some of them are skipped altogether. For example, you may not have kissed your second boyfriend until your fifth or sixth date. But now you're ready to kiss after the first or second date.

The Bible urges us not to let anything master us (1 Corinthians 6:12). But you are obviously being mastered by your desire for intimacy. In addition, your relationships are shallow because your focus is not on getting to know your date as a person but on the physical attraction. You have little motivation to work out difficulties that might increase depth and lead toward marriage.

You must break the mastery of your sexual desire and restore your sexual integrity. How? Take a sabbatical from dating. Do not place yourself in a position to become intimately involved with anyone until you have come to a point of insight, understanding, and control in your behavior. Since issues of forgiveness and control are involved, call upon the Great Healer to do what you cannot do on your own. When you feel restored and strong, slowly and wisely begin dating again.

Am I okay if I'm not interested in sex?

Every person's sex drive is different. There is nothing wrong if it isn't really important to you. If it bothers you, let's schedule an appointment for you with our physician and let him give you a checkup.

Questions About Conception and Contraception

Why can't some people make a baby?

There are many problems that cause infertility. A good physician can pinpoint the problem most of the time and suggest ways it can be corrected.

What is artificial insemination?

Artificial insemination involves taking the sperm from a fertile man (usually by masturbation) and inserting it into the uterus of a woman who is in the ovulatory stage of her cycle.

What is a test-tube baby (in vitro fertilization)?

The egg from the mother and the sperm from the father join together outside the body of the mother in a laboratory, and the resulting embryo is then returned to the uterus where it implants.

We're planning to get married. How can we know what kind of birth control is right for us?

There are many options including pills, foam, and condoms. Visit a clinic or doctor to determine the specific birth control devices to use.

Do contraceptives affect sexual pleasure?

Some of the more cumbersome methods do. But they can be incorporated into the lovemaking to offset the distraction of using them. The pill has no effect, which is one reason why people prefer it.

How safe are condoms?

If they are used correctly, leaving room at the tip and removing them as soon as ejaculation occurs, they are about 85 percent effective.

What is "safe sex"?

There is no such thing. There is "safer sex" in that the chance of pregnancy and disease are somewhat reduced by using condoms and avoiding certain sexual practices in which body fluids are easily transferred. The only way to know for certain you won't get pregnant, get someone else pregnant, or get a disease is not to be sexually intimate.

Is withdrawal a good birth control method?

Withdrawal is a poor method of birth control because of the self-control necessary to interrupt sex at the height of arousal and because sperm are often in the fluid that is released before ejaculation.

My boyfriend said that if we slip up, I can go to the doctor and get a "day after" pill or shot.

There is a medication that is used in special situations such as rape. However, it is very potent and makes the person ill. If pregnancy is not prevented, the medication can cause birth defects, particularly in the second generation. It is clearly not a solution to the consequences of premarital sex. Knowing your values and having a plan to maintain them is.

What should a couple do if things are not going well sexually?

Good sexual functioning is the result of a couple sharing intimacy and loving feelings. Technique is the easy part. Like anything else, practice helps—as long as it is accompanied by good communication. Often sex is less than expected because the couple doesn't know how to share their needs with each other. Sometimes a responsible third party can help point out better ways of communicating. After a year, if things are still not as they should be, the couple should seek professional help.

If an abortion is performed early enough, the "blob" is not a real baby, right?

Very few people believe that a baby is not a human life from the moment of conception. Improved technology continues to lower the age at which fetal organs begin to function. The heart, for example, is beating 18 days after conception. Most women cannot even tell that they are pregnant by then. The real question is are we ever justified in taking an innocent life? (See Chapter 13 for further discussion of abortion.)

PART 3

Special Issues
of Sex Education

10

Is the School Your Ally or Your Adversary?

I had just finished a talk on female sexuality when a young, well-dressed mother caught my arm. "Can I have a minute of your time?" she asked politely. Her expression revealed an urgency in her request.

"What's on your mind?" I asked.

The words tumbled out. "My children are in a local public school where they are required to take sex education. I'm so upset. Do you know what our school is teaching?" Judging by her level of agitation, I assumed the school was promoting homosexuality as a legitimate alternative lifestyle, the joys of cohabitation, or the necessity of doing what "feels" right. I was wrong. "They are making my children learn the correct names for their privates!" she announced indignantly, hands in the air for emphasis.

Maybe I'm slow, but I've yet to understand the superior wisdom some parents find in referring to genitals as "wee-wee," "Betty," or "twinkler." Teaching our children the correct terminology for all their body parts, including the genitals, is vital to their having a common frame of reference for speaking to their teachers, doctors, and spouses. This mother's concern is rather low on my list of concerns for school sex education programs.

But how far should school programs go toward educating our children about sex and sexuality? What should they include? What should they omit? A major stumbling block many parents encounter with sex education in the home or school is the misconception that it means a graphic description of sexual technique. By contrast, the primary task of sex education is to provide the context for our children's understanding of their God-given sexuality. Their understanding of who they are as males or females helps them resist social pressure, solve relational problems, and recognize the truth in a society which is often confused about sex.

Perhaps a better term for sex education would be *sexuality* education or *family life* education—any term that helps us understand that we are speaking of more than how to have sex or how to have sex without consequences! That some form of sex education is necessary is agreed upon by the vast majority of people in the United States. Every Gallup poll since the 1970s has reported 75-80 percent of all parents favoring it.

Hopefully this book is making clear to you that, whether or not sex education is presented in your child's school, you are by far the most influential sex educator your child will ever have. But many parents feel inadequate talking with their children about sex. They are too busy or too uncomfortable, or they just panic at the thought of discussing sex with their children. Some parents are confused about their own beliefs, feelings, and attitudes about sex. (After all, who modeled healthy conversations about sex or helped them verbalize and clarify their values?) Many parents resist talking about sex for fear of a potential conflict with their kids over those same beliefs, feelings, and attitudes. So parents often shift the weight of responsibility for their child's sex education from themselves to the public school.

Every parent must be diligent about monitoring public sex education programs. Any good sexuality program should have a parent component to it—and you need to participate!

The Value of Moral Value

There is no such thing as valueless sex education despite those who argue to the contrary. Teaching teens not to get pregnant by using contraceptives is as value-laden as teaching them not to have sex. Yet abstinence-based programs are rejected as narrow and moralizing while "safe sex" programs portray themselves as value-free. In reality, both programs promote certain values.

Many people say that sex education in the schools won't work because we can never agree on the values that must be presented. This is simply not true. Right-thinking, healthy people of all persuasions have many commonalities. Consider the following values most people share:

1. Sex education is a lifelong process.

2. Sex is more than a physical act.

3. A working knowledge of sex is important for everyone.

4. Every individual needs to clarify his or her personal value system.

5. A positive self-concept is essential to making responsible decisions.

6. Sexual decisions have consequences and affect lives immensely.

7. Decisions made sexually must support the dignity, quality, and worth of each person.

8. Sexual decisions must take into account the medical, psychological, and social effects of sexual activity.

9. It is wrong to exploit or force anyone sexually.

10. It is wrong to spread disease.

11. It is undesirable to bring a child into the world who is unwanted and who cannot be responsibly cared for.

12. Abortion is not a method of birth control.

13. Parenthood is rife with far more responsibilities than an adolescent can assume or is capable of.

14. Abortion is not the solution for unwanted pregnancy.

15. Parents are the primary sex educators of their children with other sources being supplemental.

16. It is healthy for children to be able to discuss their

sexual and reproductive health with parents and other trust-worthy adults.

17. Abstinence is a viable and preferred approach to teen-age sex involvement.

18. Parents and others from the community should together develop formal programs.

19. All programs should be undergirded with a message of what is important and not important, good and bad, right and wrong.

20. Sex education programs should be voluntary.

21. Sex education instructors should be trained and screened for balance and healthy attitudes.

22. Because of the diversity in a democratic society a variety of beliefs is expected and must be shown respect.[1]

"But," some may argue, "you can't tell me everyone agrees on abortion! Why did you include it on the list?" Unfortunately even Christians disagree. However, no right-thinking individual can believe that abortion is a desirable way to handle teen pregnancy, even if they take the stand based strictly on the medical health of the teen. Never having to face the decision to abort a fetus is in the best interest of the teen emotionally, socially, and medically.

No Values, No Impact

Others may persist, "You'll never get anyone to agree on what is important, right, or good!" We may not agree on all absolutes, but we must agree on some. Most of this list of values represents what decent human beings innately know is true. To leave out absolutes is to guarantee a program that is for all intents and purposes ineffective and meaningless. How do I know? Research confirms that sex education programs that are not taught within a social, values-laden format do nothing to prevent or encourage premarital sexual activity, increase the use of birth control, impact self-concept, or prevent pregnancy.

Major studies reviewing sex education literature verify that sex education classes based on information only and those with information plus pregnancy prevention by use of birth control simply do not do the job.[2] *Valueless sex educa-tion programs simply don't make a difference.*

Sex education does increase knowledge. That's good. Knowledge, however, has little impact on behavior. You've experienced that yourself. You *know* that a meal of chicken-fried steak, mashed potatoes dripping in butter, and pecan pie is a one-way trip to Cholesterol City, but you eat it anyway. You *know* that you should signal every time you change lanes, but you don't always signal. Similarly, simply informing teens that they will get pregnant if they have intercourse does not necessarily prevent them from getting involved, even when they don't plan on having sex.

Without personal values on which to base their decisions, teens are at the mercy of all kinds of social and emotional pressures which affect their reasoning. Some respond to the media's invitation to flex their sexual muscles and enjoy more immediate gratification. For others, the desire for a boyfriend or girlfriend as tangible proof of their attractiveness easily overpowers any logic not to have sex. When these factors are combined with a lack of planning for the future, a feeling that they have no personal impact on their destiny, and no church influence, simply knowing about the perils and pitfalls of premature sexual activity carries little clout in their decision-making.

Don't Do It, but If You Do ...

Another reason many school-based sex education pro-grams have failed is that most have sent a mixed message. Many programs tell kids not to get sexually involved, then say, "But if you do, here are some contraceptive options you should consider." Experience has taught us in other arenas that if you want to stay dry, you'd better not go near the water. Alcoholics Anonymous learned years ago that there is no such thing as a "social-drinking" alcoholic; a complete break with alcohol is essential to recovery. Former drug addicts discover the hard way that trying control of the amount of drugs used doesn't work. Control over addictive substances is main-tained only by an all-or-nothing approach.

Saying to an alcohol- or drug-abusing teenager, "Just say no, but if you must say yes, at least be wise," sends a mixed message that makes it easy for him to escalate his addiction. Similarly, teaching abstinence with the clause, "if you must, be wise," has proven to be equally confusing and ineffective when attempting to get teens to be sexually responsible.

Evaluating Your School's Program

How then do you know if your school-based sex education program is effective? Consider the following questions:

- Does the program take into consideration, and assist teens in maximizing, their future relationships, their sense of identity, and their control over their lives?
- Does the program strengthen the individual's belief and value systems?
- Is the program sensitive to the fact that teens are not inexperienced adults but instead are limited by their developmental capacity as well as their lack of education?

Good sex programs reinforce healthy value systems and address how to care for and be emotionally intimate with persons of both sexes. They teach the consequences of pre-marital sexual activity—pregnancy, birth, and STDs—and should reduce the possibility of early sexual involvement and unwanted pregnancy. Good instruction will increase the child's ability to communicate about sex in a clear and open manner.

Good programs are flexible enough to incorporate cultural norms and circumstances, especially those that are deterrents to pregnancy. Since strategies should focus on avoidance of sexual involvement and experimentation, timely intervention is important. By late adolescence most programs are no longer relevant.[3]

So, should you march against school-based sex education in your town? I suggest that you don't waste your energy. Instead, polish your own skills so you're up to the task of being the number one sexuality educator in your home. Then look at the approach your community programs are taking. If they aren't abstinence-based and taught by competent professionals, don't just stand there and stomp your foot! Show the administration and/or school board the secular studies that support your stand, and give them a list of available abstinence-based programs that have already proven effective. Here are some examples:

- *In God's Image: Male and Female: A Catholic Vision of Human Sexuality*, Patricia F. Miller, Franciscan Communications, 1229 S. Santee Street, Los Angeles, CA 90015, (800) 421-8510.

- *The Challenge Program*, Educational Guidance Institute, Inc., 927 S. Walter Reed Drive, Suite 4, Arlington, VA 22204, (703) 486-8313.

- *Postponing Sexual Involvement*, Emory/Grady Teen Services Program, Box 26158, Grady Memorial Hospital, 80 Butler Street S.E., Atlanta, GA 30335.

- *Teen-Aid Inc.*, W. 22 Mission, Spokane, WA 99201-2320, (509) 466-8679.

- *Sex Respect*, Coleen Mast, Respect, Inc., 347 South Center, Bradley, IL 60915, (815) 932-8389.

- *Womanity*, 2141 Youngs Valley Road, Walnut Creek, CA 94596.

- The program of the San Antonio Crisis Pregnancy Centers, 5480 Walzem Road, San Antonio, TX 78218, (512) 655-3426.

- *God's Gift of Sexuality*, Presbyterian and Reformed Educational Ministry, Curriculum Services Department, 100 Witherspoon Street, Louisville, KY 40202-1396. (I have not seen all aspects of this program. Ask questions about it that are directly pertinent to your sex education values.)

The sex education of your children is vital. If you don't know what your school is doing, find out. If the school's program violates your values and contradicts your approach to sex education, get involved and work for responsible change. Remember: Where *your* kids are concerned, you are in charge.

11

Disabled Kids Are Sexual Too

Marcus was a charming young man whose wheelchair seemed a mere annoyance. Everyone was pleased when Beth announced her decision to marry him. Two weeks after the wedding, however, Beth was back in her parents' home. The problem? Marcus' sex education had consisted of X-rated videos. His approach to his new bride was modeled after what he had seen. She was humiliated, degraded, and shocked by his insensitivity and heretofore unrecognized prurient side.

When his pastor confronted him about his callous behavior, Marcus was confused. What other way was there to treat a woman sexually? No one had offered him an alternative. His limited dating and interaction with peers had given him little opportunity to learn the subtleties of touch and unfolding eroticism. And he had certainly never heard a sermon on marital love!

Leaving the Disabled in the Dark

Should we be surprised at Marcus' dilemma? Are we parents

165

responsible when our physically disabled children grow up sexually ignorant or slow? Children with disabilities are limited in what they can seek out and experience on their own. They often lack the interaction with peers that able-bodied kids take for granted. Sometimes their diminished social skills leave them further behind other children emotionally. As in Marcus' case, what disabled children see on TV often becomes their model for life—and we have already discussed how the media has distorted the healthy concepts of love, dating, marriage, sex, and family!

The sexuality of the child who is physically and mentally challenged is routinely ignored. Why? Because there are many misconceptions about the sexual needs and capabilities of the disabled. For the most part, physical or mental disabilities are seen as rendering the person asexual. Good appearance and good health are considered synonymous with sexual attractiveness and interest.

Disabled children and adults are not only ignored, they are often sexually victimized. The rate of rape and molestation among the disabled is many times that of the general population. How can this be?

First, the disabled are devalued. It is easy for the victimizer to convince himself that what happens to disabled people doesn't matter.

Second, the disabled are vulnerable. Many are in the care of institutions, care-givers, or parents. Some disabled, conceding their physical and emotional need, are anxious to please. Previous rejections make the individual long for someone who does not appear repulsed at their appearance or behavior.

Finally, having received no warning or instruction, the disabled don't know how, or are unable, to protect themselves from sexual assault. And when something does happen they are sometimes unable to communicate with clarity or believability that they have been sexually victimized.

Pedophiles and those who can't manage adult relationships are often hired for the demanding, low-paying jobs of caring for the disabled. The helplessness of their charges appeals to them and encourages them to molestation, especially when the bathing and care of the disabled child's genitals are involved.

The truth is, no matter how incapacitated a child may be physically or mentally, he or she is by very nature a sexual being. The able-bodied and the disabled both grow up in a world full of conflicting messages about sex. In most cases they share the same desires. For each, the development of healthy sexual attitudes and behaviors results from a combination of factors, of which not least in importance is a personal value system that gives meaning and significance to sex.

Physical Health and Sexual Health

Studies reinforce the correlation between a disabled person's sense of attractiveness, sense of ability to function as a male or female, and sense of independence with being able to participate actively as a sexual partner. Those who fail to see themselves as healthy, sexual beings are more apt to suppress sexual possibilities, are more preoccupied with their own bodies and physical complaints, and are less successfully rehabilitated. Consequently they suffer more depression, greater anxiety, decreased self-worth, difficulties with relationships, and poorer vocational adjustments. Ignoring the sexual component of a disabled child's life can affect his ability to cope successfully in other areas of his life.

The Prospect of a Healthy Sex Life

When we think of children with disabilities, we tend to think of them as being completely unable to carry on sexual relationships as adults. Yet the percentage of disabled adults whose troubles preclude the possibility of a sexual relationship is actually quite small. Sexual functioning is as important to the disabled who choose to marry as it is to any married couple.

A high percentage of male spinal cord victims are able to

have reflex erections, and recent advances have made it possible for them to father children. Secondary erogenous zones are common in disabled males as are physiological referral orgasms in some women. Cord-injured women can and do report orgasm despite complete loss and denervation of genital sensation. With multiple sclerosis, spina bifida, and the like, the chief frustration is often dealing with bowel and urinary conditions. Honest communication about sexual needs and desires is as vital to the disabled couple as to the able-bodied.

The concept of healthy, successful sexuality of necessity must not be locked into a particular physical scenario for the disabled. As with the able-bodied, the emotional significance of a sexual encounter is where the emphasis should lie. The purposes of sex—mutual pleasure, increased self-worth, and greater intimacy—can even be achieved by the disabled when they adopt this broader, biblical understanding of the sex act.

The Bible does not require that couples include certain activities or follow a prescribed order in lovemaking. It is man-made thinking that suggests that within marriage certain types of sexual expression are sanctioned and others are not or that physical response is the measure of great sex. The disabled couple can be very creative in learning how to stimulate and fulfill each other sexually.

I like to compare a couple's available sexual choices to a sumptuous buffet. We relish buffets for their variety. Even the pickiest person can find some items on the table that suit his appetite—and he can heap them on his plate in proportions that suit his capacity. Enjoyment results no matter what choices are made or in what order the food is eaten.

It is difficult for many parents to envision their children married and sexually active. Although disabled persons of dating age need closeness as much as other single adults, many parents fear that their disabled offspring will be hurt in a romantic relationship. In actuality everyone risks being hurt in the process of dating and marrying!

What's a parent to do? How much the disabled child is encouraged and allowed to date is a very personal and private decision each family must make. Individual family situations and values and the child's ability to function all go into determining the correct thing to do. Realistic education and counseling are essential if marriage is desired. Marriage is hard for anyone!

Sex Education for the Disabled Child

There is no question that sex education is appropriate for children with disabilities. Studies indicate that sex education programs for adolescents with mental handicaps and other disabilities can be successful in imparting knowledge, changing attitudes, and fostering openness.[1] Without such programs, or when they are delayed, problems escalate.[2] Sexuality education enriches the lives of challenged youngsters through their expanded knowledge and improved sense of self-worth. It increases social acceptance and mobility by reinforcing responsible behavior. Guilt, fear, and anxiety are reduced. Most important, it provides some protection against exploitation.

Dorothy Clark is well known for her work with the developmentally disabled at Walnut Creek Presbyterian Church in northern California. It was business as usual for her when a local pastor called to report a "serious" incident. A mildly retarded boy at his church simply couldn't keep his hands off the girls. The pastor was at a loss. What was he to do? He thought he had better go to the parents, but did Dorothy agree?

Dorothy calmly asked the usually competent man what he would do if the boy was of normal intelligence. There was a pause, and an almost visible light bulb went on. "Of course!" he laughed aloud. "If it were anyone else I would speak directly to him and teach more appropriate behavior."

Our prejudice sometimes gets in the way of the obvious. The only difference when educating the mentally disabled is that the lessons need to be simple and direct and probably will need repeating. Role-playing appropriate behavior is very helpful. The hugs and kisses that the young Down's child, for example, lavishes on friends and strangers alike are inappropriate as he or she ages. Such actions may make him or her vulnerable to abuse. But even mentally retarded youngsters can be taught acceptable ways to relate in social situations.

Bobby seemed oblivious to such social graces. He enraptured his classmates by violently beating his penis until an erection occurred. The usual repetitive training had not made a dent in his behavior. Then social workers discovered that Bobby had few social or recreational outlets. He knew only one way to be the center of attention. His behavior was changed when those caring for him helped him master skills that were more appropriate. Sometimes it is necessary to look at the motivation rather than the act alone.

Parents often react negatively to masturbation in a normal child. With the slow child they panic. Normal kids are expected to date, socialize, make jokes about sex, and do some experimenting. Not so for the disabled. For them the love, support, and teaching that leads to healthy sexuality is replaced with conflicting messages. Their parents, burdened by an already overwhelming responsibility, are not anxious to open the door on the complexity of sexuality. Indeed it is difficult to work with a child who may have a limited understanding of biology, a difficult time delaying gratification, and/or whose sense of alienation and inferiority leaves him hungry for greater dependence and affection.

Our general aversion to facing sexual issues is simply magnified with the disabled child. Because of our reluctance, some children with disabilities transition toward handicap as a way of life. They function with little sense of self-worth and increasingly pull away from others. Social isolation leads to despair. Being in touch emotionally and physically with others is a necessary first step to becoming a healthy sexual person.

No matter what the condition of a child's body or mind, we are to accept that child as the sexual boy or girl, man or woman God made him or her to be. Sexuality is part of the total package of the child's personhood and identity. As we minister to the whole child by including loving sexuality education, "then will the lame leap like a deer" (Isaiah 35:6).

12

It Shouldn't Hurt to Be a Kid

As an aware, concerned parent, Debra was determined to protect her two-year-old from sexual molestation or abuse. She and her husband carefully explained to little Heather about her privates and admonished her to tell them if anyone ever touched her there.

Several days passed before the couple was assured that Heather had gotten the message. Sensing the seriousness with which the lesson had been taught, an equally sober Heather walked into the kitchen and dutifully reported to her parents, "C.J. licked my privates today." The couple eyed each other and smiled discreetly, assured that Heather had learned her lesson under relatively harmless circumstances. C.J. was the family dog.

No child is excluded from the horrible possibility of being exploited by people whose upbringing fostered unhealthy and unholy perspectives of sex. Sadly, many children learn about sexual abuse the hard way because their parents aren't as conscientious as Heather's parents. Besides reducing the possibility of early sexual involvement and the myriad of repercussions that follow it, the sexuality education of your children will hopefully protect them from sexual abuse, molestation, and exploitation. Furthermore, your attentiveness to the issue of sexual abuse will equip you to minister to your children's friends and playmates, and to their parents as well.

Sexual Abuse:
The Sobering Reality

Fortunately, we are learning how common sexual abuse of children is and discovering ways to prevent it. Babies and preschoolers aren't immune to this tragedy, but the school-age child is particularly vulnerable. It's happening in your neighborhood whatever socioeconomic level it represents. Children are abused most frequently by people they know and have reason to trust.

Abuse exists in families in which relationships have become distorted and confused. Frequently alcohol is a factor. Although devastating for all involved, the child often goes unsupported, particularly by the mother. Often even the courts fail to support the child, as illustrated by the recent jailing of a girl who refused to testify against her father.

Kids under 16 years old make up one-third of all sex abuse victims. Young boys are at greatest risk at ages six and seven and young girls at two stages: five and six and 14 and 15. Both sexes are mainly abused by males; females only account for 4 percent of all incidents of abuse. Often the male abuser is young, a loner, passive and withdrawn, poor in school, and immature socially and sexually. Almost half of the occurrences of abuse happen in the child's own home, the home of the assailant, or at school.[1]

Some children are at greater risk than others. Children with stepfathers are five times more likely to be abused (not necessarily always by the stepfather, however). In a home without a mother, the risk of abuse is tripled. The emotional needs of the child in such homes makes them especially vulnerable. Fathers who have insisted on strict obedience and subordination of females in the family increase the risk of abuse. So do parents who hold strict attitudes about sex, severely punishing children for such acts as masturbating or viewing lewd materials. But parents who have been abused themselves as children run the highest risk of being sexually abusive.[2]

Forty percent of all sexual abuse occurs between close family members. Many such families are dysfunctional. They are skilled at looking good on the outside while maintaining a conspiracy of silence about what occurs between them. Bringing incestuous relationships out in the open almost inevitably results in the dissolution of the family. More enlightened states are approaching the problem by stressing the healing of all family members through counseling.

Considerable marital stress results when a mom abdicates her role or resorts to passivity and denial. Either response places the daughter at great risk of abuse. Father-son incest is often characterized by violence, alcohol, and an impulsive, out-of-control dad. Little is known of sibling abuse, although it is common. The repercussions of it depend on whether or not there was a considerable age or power difference between the children and whether the sexual behavior was forced through fear or coercion.[3]

Telltale Signs of Abuse

Children may signal that they have been abused by exhibiting behavioral and emotional problems. They may suddenly have difficulty sleeping. Their grades may fall in school. Feeling increasingly isolated, they devalue themselves and may begin to think of suicide or running away. They may get involved in alcohol and drug abuse. The very young child may masturbate more, display sexual positions, or use language that is clearly adult in origin.

It is not uncommon for girls to react to sexual abuse by becoming sexually permissive or by shutting down their response and trust systems in future sexual relationships. The percentage of teen prostitutes who were first victims of forced sex is very high.

Running away or marrying early are ways by which teens

escape a no-win home life. Unfortunately, escape is no antidote for the pain of being violated; the problems remain. New research indicates that some abuse victims adopt multiple personalities as a coping mechanism, a phenomenon once thought to be very rare. Adaptation by acquiring a compulsive life pattern is very common. Such adaptations provide the "fix" that distracts from the emotional pain.

Women abused as children report more depression, anxiety, and low self-worth than other women. Their poor self-image is sometimes reflected in their choice of inferior men. Family relationships are often strained for these victims. It is common for sexual counseling to be needed, for many women with an abusive past find sexual adjustment in marriage very laborious. Early sexual experiences result in a greater number of problems when force was used, when sexual behavior was guilt producing, and/or when involvement was with a close family member.[4]

Sexual abuse can make a person physically ill. A study of 700 largely middle-class, well-educated women abused in childhood reported they were twice as likely to have been hospitalized as those with no such history. They had a greater number of gynecological problems, including increased susceptibility to PMS. They also struggled more with obesity, headaches, fatigue, and sleep and substance abuse problems.[5]

The Trauma of Rape

According to statistics compiled by the Senate Judiciary Committee, 16 women are confronted by rapists every hour in the United States, and a woman is raped every six minutes. With incest, which is likely to be habitual, the violation of trust runs deep and is probably the most damaging aspect. But with rape, the act often leaves the victim fearful for his or her life.

The adolescent who has been raped may develop phobias about leaving home, interacting with strangers, and pursuing relationships. After a period of denial, psychosomatic complaints occur just as they do with older victims. Male victims of rape, fearing the stigma of homosexuality and having been involved in a deviant sexual behavior, are less likely to tell anyone what happened. Trauma is increased for the female teen victim who frequently finds that when she reports what happened she receives little support, is not believed, and/or is accused of contributing to her own rape! Such attitudes have encouraged the alarming increase of date rape, especially on college campuses.

Rape is an act of violence. A rapist is an angry person whose uncontrollable rage is expressed through sexuality. A rapist is also a person whose only concern is his own satisfaction. He is an exploiter who preys on his victim's vulnerabilities.

Are rapists made or born? Unquestionably there are societal factors that contribute to a rapist mentality. The United States has a rape rate four times higher than Germany, 13 times higher than Britain, and 20 times higher than Japan.[6]

One reason our country has such a staggering rape problem is the desensitization to sexual violence we are exposed to in the media. Men who view scenes of violence toward women in movies, on TV, and in pornographic publications become desensitized to rape, demeaning practices, and violence toward females.

Furthermore, research suggests that violent and degrading depictions of sexuality result in the general public being less sympathetic toward rape victims and their psychological and physical injuries.[7] Exposure to such materials causes many people to conclude that women are responsible for preventing their own rape, that rapists should not be severely punished, and that women should resist a rape attack.[8]

An Ounce of Prevention

It is imperative that we protect our children from sexual abuse and exploitation. And since it is impossible for us to be with them all the time, we must teach them to protect themselves. My only caution is that you don't make information about sexual abuse available to them without also teaching them about God's ideal for the gift of sex. (I'm not suggesting that both topics be treated at the same time but that you make sure the message they hear is not limited to the misuse of sexuality.) Reinforce the fact that healthy sexuality has nothing to do with brutality or humiliation. It is the porno industry that has linked sex with violence; God links sex with love.

Any preventative program you, your church, or your school adopts should have five components.

1. Make sure children learn to recognize potentially dangerous situations. Don't warn children about strangers with candy. They make no connection between candy and someone touching their genitals. Be specific in your warnings so they know what molestation consists of. Then reassure them that because they know about abuse, they have a plan of action: to refuse it and leave. Help them define good touching, bad touching, and touching that confuses them or makes them uncomfortable. Most children innately sense what is wrong, but they need reinforcement that any discomfort they feel when being touched by someone else is valid.

2. Children should be taught from day one that their bodies are special and private. Each child has a right and responsibility to take care of his or her body. They must learn that protecting themselves from sexual abuse, even when perpetrated by an adult authority figure, is appropriate and sometimes necessary. Kids who don't feel valuable and special are vulnerable to the promises of eternal love, attention, and friendship the perpetrator uses to manipulate them.

3. Help your children identify one or more trustworthy adults they can talk to about incidents or attempts of sexual abuse. Also encourage them to talk among their peers about their fears, their experiences with abusers, and ways they can protect themselves. These measures will increase the chance that they will report any suspicious incidents.

It is important that children who are abused be encouraged to express their feelings about the incident by acting out or verbalizing their rage or confusion. However, don't project the anger and rage you feel about the incident onto your child. Remember: Children are incapable of understanding the significance of a sexual act from an adult standpoint. To declare to the child that he or she is "ruined" only ensures that the child will attach greater significance to what is already traumatic.

4. Teach your children that the victim of sexual abuse is never at fault and need not feel shame. I remember as a child being terrified in a movie when the man sitting next to me began to rub my leg. I had no plan of action for dealing with this violation, because I had not been warned that such a thing could happen. I instinctively grabbed my reluctant friend and rushed toward the lobby supposedly to get popcorn. I was terribly embarrassed about the incident and only grudgingly told my mother about it, fearing that I would be blamed for doing something wrong.

Isn't it interesting that the overriding response in the victim of abuse, molestation, or rape is shame? A major part of recovery from abuse is the victim's understanding that he or she is not at fault for what happened. The victim is *never* guilty. All programs or private approaches must reiterate the innocence of the abuse victim. Good counseling can uncover hidden fears, reaffirm the child as a valuable person, and give hope for the future.

5. Societal mind-sets that perpetuate the importance of power and dominance for men must be replaced. Men who take an active role in rearing their children bond with them in a way that reduces the chance that they will think of their children as objects to be used at will.

The importance of rethinking the ways we view women and children is demonstrated by the results of a long-range study concluding that sexual abuse has increased in the United States during the twentieth century. We must wonder if the increase in pornography accounts for some of the objectification and devaluing of children. Today a greater number of the perpetrators are relatives or adults known to the child, and the abuse is often of a more serious type.[9]

As much as you may want to, you can't keep your children from being exposed to potentially abusive relationships. You have no way of knowing which of their relatives, teachers, coaches, neighbors, or peers may try to exploit them sexually. But as you teach them God's design for sex and sexuality, you can be confident that your children will learn to identify and avoid that which deviates from it.

13

Hot Buttons: Homosexuality, Masturbation, Abortion, Contraception

Throughout this book I have referred to several topics related to sexuality education which are somewhat controversial in our society, even among Christians. I call these topics "hot buttons" because no matter how you touch them you're bound to set off an explosive reaction in someone!

I don't claim to be the final authority on any of these issues. But since they will inevitably come up in your family discussions of sex and sexuality, I want to add some input from my experience as a therapist which may help you deal with them when your children ask about them.

Homosexuality

There are many issues of sexuality on which the Bible is silent (such as masturbation and specific lovemaking techniques), but homosexuality is not one of them. In Genesis 19 God destroys the city of Sodom because of its inhabitants' gross unrighteousness as exemplified by their blatant homosexuality (verse 5). Sodomy, the term for anal intercourse between males, derives its name from this wicked city. In Romans 1:26-28 God's judgment is pronounced on women and men who practice homosexuality. In 1 Corinthians 6:9,10 homosexuality is listed among the sins practiced by those who will not inherit the kingdom of God (although, as verse 11 states, forgiveness is just as available for homosexuals as for other sinners). Sexual contact between two people of the same sex is clearly outside the boundaries of God's plan for His human creation.

However, the Bible's clear position on homosexuality does not excuse Christian parents from endeavoring to understand it in order to help their children separate the truth from fable and falsehood. This is my intent in the paragraphs that follow.

I have seen a number of young boys in therapy who feared they were gay (most of them weren't). They worried about it because they had been approached by another male, because they had an acquaintance or relative who was gay, or, most frequently, because they had engaged in same-sex sexual play (as 30 percent of all boys do).[1] Girls who wondered if they were homosexual had "emotional" bonds with other females which they considered impossible with a male.

Relieve anxiety for children and teens. Mention in your conversations with them how common same-sex play is and that it has no relationship with their sexual orientation. In reality, such exploration is often merely a rehearsal for future heterosexual events. Assure children who consider themselves on the borderline that they are free to choose to follow God's plan for their sexuality as the male or female He designed them to be.

If you are worried about your child's orientation, be careful that you don't inadvertently belittle one sex or the other by your attitudes or actions. Accept and teach that all people have masculine and feminine traits to some degree. Be a healthy role model. Protect your children from anyone who might misuse them. Help them learn to show love for those of the same sex in other than physical ways. Ground them in God's message of the equal importance of the two sexes, and in His design for humankind.

No scientific study has shown conclusively that same-sex orientation is due to one's genes or hormonal balance.

Instead it appears that most homosexuals choose to enter a gay lifestyle in response to a number of factors, including learning and psychological issues. The fact that multiple causes are behind a person's decision for homosexuality is probably why traditional therapists have had so little success helping gays.

Although we've often heard that distant fathers or smothering mothers are responsible for a child choosing a gay lifestyle, Dr. Elizabeth Moberly, in a thorough review of the literature, suggests the problem lies in the lack of same-sex bonding. A major factor in lesbian orientation appears to be sexual abuse, which sets up or adds to a feeling of being different. Dr. Moberly, a Christian psychologist, has devoted her time and energy to helping churches approach the homosexual in a new and healing way.[2]

There is an organization for parents who discover that their child is living a gay lifestyle. Spatula Ministry, so named because the revelation of a child's homosexuality often leaves parents in a state where they must be scraped off the ceiling, is a blessing for many.[3] For more information about Christians who have left the homosexual lifestyle or for help in finding programs, support literature, and tapes on ministry to homosexuals, Exodus International is another helpful resource.[4]

For most people, changing a behavior, a habit, or a lifestyle is a gradual process, and so it is for the homosexual who chooses to return to God's plan for his or her sexuality. There are addictive elements to deal with, personal choices to make, and insecurities to face. But the real question boils down to who is in charge. Are we blobs of protoplasm that respond only to the biological and sociological cards we were dealt, or do we have choices about the way we will live our lives? Your children must understand that the latter is the case.

Whether healing from homosexuality means complete reorientation to marriage and family or the ability to live a God-honoring lifestyle as a single, our ministry to our children or our neighbor's child must facilitate the journey. Should your child announce that he or she has chosen the gay lifestyle, remember that he or she is still God's child—the same one you loved before you knew. Barbara Johnson, founder of Spatula Ministry and the mother of a formerly gay son, reminds us that it's our job as parents to love them, and it's God's job to change them.

The AIDS Crisis

AIDS is an issue that is affecting people of all sexual orientations, not just homosexuals. But since the disease is so drastically impacting the gay community we will consider it here.

Just yesterday the headlines in our local paper announced: "AIDS will be fifth leading killer of young women by '91, study finds." Headline-making news indeed! My husband's ob-gyn medical updates speak of gynecologists being the new frontline physicians for the next generation of the disease. Despite the hope of a vaccine or other modifying drugs, over one million people are already infected. In New York and New Jersey, AIDS has already killed more women between the ages of 15 and 44 than any other health problem. Predictably, such trends portend disaster for thousands of children.

Our children need to know the facts about AIDS, and those facts can be presented in ways that are appropriate to their age and experience. Kids understand that diseases are passed from person to person. They need to know that the "germ" that causes AIDS is carried in body fluids. If those body fluids aren't directly exchanged there is little risk of getting the disease. There is no need to tell a young child the details of anal and oral sex.

Although the AIDS virus has been found in saliva, tears, breast milk, and urine, it is most frequently in blood, semen, and vaginal secretions. Not everyone who carries the AIDS virus will get the disease, but anyone who is infected is potentially capable of transmitting the virus to another person.

One of the factors that increases the odds of heterosexual transmission of AIDS is the presence of other STDs. The more sexual partners a person has, the greater the risk. Encouraging abstinence among youth is essential. The younger a teen begins to date, the more apt he or she is to become sexually active with a number of partners.

I have stated throughout this book that sex education is useless unless facts are presented within a framework of moral and social values. Teaching sexual restraint as a virtue (along with strong parenting) is even listed in the government's advice to parents on AIDS education. Additionally, we must make sure that we are available to our children to help them articulate their fears and correct their misconceptions.

Masturbation

I am not writing this passage as a pro- or anti-masturbation message. No matter what I say, 50 percent of you will probably disagree with me anyway. Such is the nature of the problem of masturbation. However, the subject needs to be approached without the customary emotionalism and certainly without the many myths and untruths that surround the usual discussions about it.

Too much time and energy is spent by people on both sides trying to come to terms with guilt and judgmentalism. I suggest that these attitudes are more from Satan's corner than from the Lord's. My major frustration stems from the fact that so much has been made out of so little. We spend hours thinking, talking, debating, and condemning something God apparently wasn't concerned enough about to mention specifically.

Remember: Each person's sexual drive is as individual as he or she is. My needs aren't the same as yours. The neighbor child's needs aren't the same as your child's needs. What for one person might be a major sexual need presents no difficulty at all for another.

Self-Pleasuring from Infancy

The normal infant will experience orgasm within the first year of life. Physically and emotionally healthy babies will find pleasure rubbing their genitals against their mother's body, rubbing their thighs together, and touching their genitals with their hands. As a baby grows, he also discovers the pleasures of another child's body against his own, sometimes innocently sexualizing his actions.

Physically or emotionally deprived infants, however, generally do not masturbate (although young children who have been sexually molested may manifest their stress by masturbating). Instead they will rock, bang their heads, or suck their thumbs excessively. Only a healthy child involves himself or herself in genital play. The sad, emotionally withdrawn, or physically deprived child does not bother.[5]

As the child grows older, masturbation cannot be ignored; it must be addressed. You have accepted your child's sexuality since birth. Now accept how he chooses to be sexual. View sexuality from the child's perspective; he in no way fantasizes his actions as adults do. Children are easily distracted from masturbation patterns that are due to boredom or the need for comfort.

Masturbation requires social manners as the child grows older. Some parents find it a challenge to affirm to their children that God made their bodies capable of feeling good, while at the same time teaching them to limit the enjoyment of those sensations to healthy and socially approved behaviors. Just as we teach our children manners in all other areas of life, we must also teach them manners in reference to their self-pleasuring. For example, you may say, "Touching yourself there feels very good, but bringing pleasure to ourselves is something we do in private in the bathroom or in our rooms."

By age 15 or 16 the majority of boys have masturbated. The figures reach 98 percent among college-age males and 65-80 percent among college-age females.[6] It is so universally experienced by youth, we might wonder about the teenage male who hasn't explored his sexuality to this degree.

Right or Wrong?

We have created a dilemma with masturbation. Credibility is deservedly questioned when we maintain that the most vile and dire things will befall us should we succumb to it—but we have and they didn't! In fact, people who study these things tell us that a person who knows how to masturbate is more easily orgasmic within marriage.

The real question, however, is whether masturbation is within God's framework for us. What most Christians do agree on is that we should allow nothing to master us in the sense of it becoming an idol to us. God is to be first. Whatever we do is to glorify Him (Colossians 3:23). So now let's look at a couple of arguments that suggest masturbation is not within God's will.

First, some Christians are afraid that once begun masturbation becomes excessive and participants become entranced by it, thus making the practice idolatrous. We all know people who have idolized their job, money, position, or ministry and failed to function well as Christians. It appears that even good things can be misused.

Few people center their lives around masturbation to the point of idolatry, however. The exception is the sex addict who in many cases uses masturbation as part of his ritual of compulsive behavior. Masturbation should be off-limits for him in the same way the social drink is not allowed to the alcoholic. For although everything is permissible, not everything is good—especially if it has mastery over you (1 Corinthians 6:12).

Second, consider the contention that masturbation is wrong because it uses singly what God intended to be shared. Can self-pleasuring ever really glorify the Lord? I don't know, but I hope so. Interestingly, we don't hear the same objections when we use our mouths, whose function is to eat and communicate, to sing a solo in the shower. I can imagine God's delight as we raise our voices in praise to Him. Don't you wonder if He might be just as pleased as we delight in, marvel at, and thank Him for having given us a body that is capable of feeling terrific (1 Timothy 4:4)?

Being within God's framework seems to depend a great deal on our attitudes. We can use our mouths to praise the Lord and curse our brother, eat until full or be gluttonous.

Our thoughts can be positive and loving or hateful and violent. And most decidedly, our bodies can be used to celebrate life or denigrate it. Unlike gluttony and gossip, however, which are specifically mentioned, anything about masturbation must be extrapolated from the Scriptures. For example, masturbation in adults that involves fantasy—as it almost always does—would fall under the specific condemnation of lust (Matthew 5:27,28).

Yet we must consider if perhaps such sexual release was planned for others besides youngsters. Maybe it is a real alternative for adolescents who lack the emotional maturity to make a lifelong commitment, for the single, for the divorced or widowed, or for those with ill spouses. You may feel comfortable with your personal decision to leave masturbation in your childhood, but are any of us really so sure, given the lack of specifics, that we know what is comfortable for anyone else?

Perusing Christian literature, you will find masturbation categorized as everything from a fleshly lust, a less than ideal standard, or a legitimate way to release sexual tension to a wise provision. Clearly, indulging in masturbation ourselves and advising our children what to do should be governed by the motivation of our heart, whether our personalities and habits place us in danger of idolizing it or being mastered by it, and whether we interpret Scripture in any way to preclude it. Romans 14 is a good passage to review for anyone struggling with the acceptability of this issue. We can be sure that the Lord knows our struggle, and nothing will separate us from His love.

Abortion

My normally rather easygoing daughter Malika becomes impassioned when defending her stand against abortion. Judging by the arrests, bombings, and harassment we see on both sides of the issue, abortion is a subject filled with passion for many people. Perhaps your own family is a microcosm of what is going on in the streets!

As a therapist I'm painfully aware that once an unplanned pregnancy has occurred there is no best way to handle the dilemma. There is no quick fix when God's best hasn't been chosen first.

It is no surprise that schools avoid the issue of abortion. And yet it has been stated that the most dangerous place to be today is in a mother's womb. Since 1973, when abortion was legalized, 20 million babies have been aborted. By comparison, only about 59,000 Americans were killed in the entire Vietnam war.[7]

In 1978 the teenage abortion rate was 644 for every 1000 live births.[8] Most abortions are performed at eight weeks. At two-and-one-half weeks there is a detectable heartbeat. Brain waves are evident at five-and-one-half weeks. Counsel to the adolescent must relate that medical procedures are eliminating more than cells or blobs. No one can make a wise decision based on half-truths.

If you are not aware of the long-term effects of abortion, familiarize yourself with post-abortion syndrome. This is an identifiable syndrome that tends to come to light years after an abortion. What appears to be a face-saving, clean way to take care of a problem of inconvenient and/or awkward timing has lifelong ramifications, especially for those who felt there was no viable alternative. It is obvious that adolescents need practical support if they choose not to take what only appears to be the easy way out of an unplanned pregnancy.

It is not my purpose here to present all the medical and biblical arguments concerning the right to life. I do challenge you to drop the rhetoric and look at the facts. Recent medical techniques have given us glimpses at the newly conceived fetus never available before. The humanity of these individuals is evident. The years since abortion was legalized have revealed the emotional, personal, and social price women pay for aborting an unborn child. The truth speaks for itself; have you dared to consider it?

Adoption: Fun and Games

One of the alternatives to abortion is giving the child up for adoption. Our daughter Malika is adopted. She became part of our family when she was six months old. I remember fondly the day she announced to me, after my tirade on the long list of chores she still had to do, that she had been adopted for "fun and games" and having to work wasn't part of the deal. I squelched the laughter just long enough to clarify that adoption meant she was one of the family and thus had the same responsibilities as the rest of us. Today it is generally accepted that growing up knowing you are adopted is far less traumatic than finding out at a later date or by accident.

When she was younger, Malika fantasized about meeting her birth-mother (the terms "birth-mother" and "mother who gave you your birthday" are helpful with adopted children). I assured her that when she became an adult, she would be welcome to do that. In the meantime, she's my daughter and I'm her mother. Most of the time, despite the fact that she is the only one in our family with the brunet hair and the gorgeous tan (she's Filipino), I don't think about her being adopted.

Children are four or five years old before they can truly understand what adoption means. Malika frequently referred to growing inside me long after she understood she was adopted. Giving up her fantasy required her to come to terms with having been relinquished by one mother and the possibility of it happening again with her second mother.

We never denied Malika's adoption, but we did allow her to accept it at her own pace. Naturally there was a lot of reassurance about the permanence of our situation. Carole Livingston's book, *Why Was I Adopted?*, continues to be a help to us. Another resource is Kay Marshall Strom's book for parents, *Chosen Families*, which includes a story about adoption for children.

Contraception

Eighty percent of our sexually active teenagers fail to use birth control.[9] The only teens who consistently use contraception are those who are very active or are in stable relationships. Having birth control information is not the determining factor in a teen's becoming sexually active.

Given the controversial nature of birth control, it is no wonder that thoughts of providing it to adolescents produce heart palpitations. Giving birth control devices implies approval. It leaves nothing for the child to aspire to, and it adds to the already overwhelming pitch by our culture to be sexual.

I see no advantage to the practice of supplying contraceptive devices "just in case." If, however, my son or daughter came to me and shared his or her intention to begin sexual relations against God's will and mine, my first response would be to thank God for allowing good enough communication between us so I had another chance to help him or her evaluate the motivation and reinforce God's desires. My second response would be to remind him or her to seek proper medical advice. Babies who give birth to babies risk having premature children with greater than normal chances of retardation and birth defects. Statistics further show that adolescent parents have less stable marriages, have more children, and have them closer together, often abusing them. They also have less education, resulting in less advancement in life. Tragically, the suicide rate, already second only to accidents among teens as a cause of death, escalates among unmarried pregnant girls.

Why don't teens use contraceptives? The answer isn't as obvious as them not knowing about such devices. They lack the cognitive-emotional development to understand the power of future consequences. They don't believe pregnancy can happen to them. Thus they are willing to take chances.

Also, unwillingness to admit they are sexually active precludes advance planning. Girls especially prefer that it "just happened" because that sounds more romantic. It's not hard to see that if we raise our teens to accept themselves as sexual creatures capable of powerful physical desires over which they have control, much of this line of thinking will simply not have credibility with them.

Some teenage girls set out to become pregnant. Pregnancy is seen as a resolution to all kinds of personal problems. Again, their cognitive immaturity prevents them from understanding how they actually magnify their predicament with pregnancy. Girls who make such a choice often have very difficult home lives or lack a good relationship with their father. They seek love, touch, and approval from someone else as a substitute.

The only birth control method that always works is abstinence. It is a mistake to suggest to teens that the only problem with teenage sexual involvement is pregnancy. Perhaps in this age of AIDS, abortion, and marriages racked with sexual problems acquired from past sexual partners, pregnancy is the least of the worries!

14

Are You a Well-grounded Parent?

D o you feel encouraged, equipped, and motivated for helping your child discover "the facts of life"? I hope so. There is simply too much at stake to leave the education of our children to happenstance. Yes, you and I did muddle through. But the chances that our children will "luck out" as we did are slim to none. We did not have to cope with the onslaught of sexual pressures that face the kids of the '90s. Divorce has undermined the foundation of the haven from which life could be faced. For many the belief system that enabled a child to make decisions based on the premise that there are higher values has been replaced with situational ethics.

Because sexual pressures on children are great and the ramifications of our sex-crazed culture are far-reaching, giving your child a good sexuality education is a gift of immeasurable worth. Minimally, what do you need to do? First, make a commitment that, even if it is not from you, your child will have access to healthy and correct information about his or her body and its normal functions. Second, provide an atmosphere in which your children (and maybe the neighbor's children as well) feel free to discuss, ask questions, and think through moral sexual dilemmas. Last, do what you can to get your own sexual life in order so that your influence will be reinforced not only by what you say but how you live. In truth, I would put the third point first, but that's asking a lot from those of you who have been the victims of inappropriate or hurtful sexual experiences.

What's the worst thing you could do in regard to your child's sexuality education? Let your child believe the world's message—that sex is a recreational, physical experience with no further meaning or significance. If you remain silent, that's the message they will receive. Oh yes, they will eventually learn the truth. But the price they will pay physically, socially, emotionally, and spiritually will be great—and some may never fully recover.

If anything I have said in this book has left an impression, I hope it's that your job as a sex educator is not over after your obligatory one-shot discussion of the birds and the bees. I hope you realize that your influence and your availability as a resource are a lifetime contribution to your child's sexual development. You are not merely expounding a few facts. You are setting a tone for living that will follow your son or daughter for life.

The enormity of the task and our desire to do it well reinforce our need to approach sex education with intelligence, calmness, and an overall plan. Obviously we can never be successful on our own. We must use the power of God consistently for guidance and support.

We need to be well-grounded parents. We speak of being grounded in the Word of God—knowing the Bible so well that we incorporate its principles into every aspect of our lives. We must also be grounded in our sexual knowledge and in a plan for communicating God's idea of sex and sexuality to our children. The following summarizes what it means to be a well-grounded parent: God has a plan. We must recognize our responsibility to implement His plan by being open with our children and by modeling God's plan of sexuality for them so that unhealthy influences will be mediated, so that they will incorporate God's desires for their sexual lives in a natural and normal way, and so that they do not succumb to the world. We must educate ourselves biblically and scientifically, developing a plan we can use during our child's entire life.

Notes

Chapter 2

1. "Neilsen Report Gets the Picture on Generation Gap," *Los Angeles Times* (June 11, 1990).
2. Leslie J. Chamberlin, "Sex and Today's Children," *Clearing House*, vol. 54, no. 9 (May 1981), p. 414.
3. Carol A. Darling and Mary W. Hicks, "Parental Influence on Adolescent Sexuality: Implications for Parents as Educators," *Journal of Youth and Adolescence*, vol. 11, no. 3 (June 1982), pp. 131-45.
4. Marlena Studer and Arland Thornton, "Adolescent Religiosity and Contraceptive Usage," *Journal of Marriage and the Family*, vol. 49, no. 1 (February 1987), p. 122.
5. Sally Koblinsky and Jean Atkinson, "Parental Plans for Children's Sex Education," *Family Relations* (January 1982), pp. 29-35.
6. Greer Litton Fox, "The Mother-Adolescent Daughter Relationship as a Sexual Socialization Structure: A Research Review," *Family Relations* (January 1980), pp. 21-27.
7. Koblinsky and Atkinson, "Parental Plans."
8. Darling and Hicks, "Parental Influence on Adolescent Sexuality."
9. Ibid.
10. J.F. Kantner and M. Zelnik, "Sexual Experiences of Young Unmarried Women in the U.S.," *Family Planning Perspectives*, vol. 4 (1972), pp. 9-18.
11. Elizabeth Thomson, "Socialization for Sexual Contraceptive Behavior: Moral Absolutes Versus Relative Consequences," *Youth and Society*, vol. 14, no. 1 (September 1982), pp. 103-28.

Chapter 3

1. Ronald G. Walters, *Primers for Prudery: Sexual Advice to Victorian America* (Englewood Cliffs, NJ: Prentice-Hall, 1974), pp. 1-2.

Chapter 4

1. C. Safran, "Why Religious Women Are Good Lovers," *Redbook*, vol. 146, no. 103 (April 1976), pp. 103, 155-56, 158-59.
2. Laura Shapiro, "Guns and Dolls," *Newsweek* (May 28, 1990), pp. 56-65.

Chapter 6

1. Doris Golden, "Children Have a Right to Know," *Journal of National Sex Education Week*, vol. 1 (October 1978), p. 38.

Chapter 7

1. Luis T. Garcia, "Exposure to Pornography and Attitudes about Women and Rape: A Correlation Study," *Journal of Sex Research*, vol. 22, no. 3 (August 1986), p. 382.
2. Allie C. Kilpatrick, "Some Correlates of Women's Childhood Sexual Experiences: A Retrospective Study," *Journal of Sex Research*, vol. 22, no. 2 (May 1986), p. 239.

Chapter 8

1. Richard Durfield, PhD., "For Wedlock Only." Contact: For Wedlock Only, 1407 Foothill Blvd., Suite 307, LaVerne, CA 91750, (714) 592-5262.

Chapter 9

1. Carolyn Koons and Harold Ivan Smith, seminar for singles (Tampa, 1983).
2. Ibid.

Chapter 10

1. Peter Scales, PhD., "Sexuality Education: The Value of Values," *Planned Parenthood, Emphasis Subscriber Services*, 810 Seventh Avenue, New York, NY 10019. Christians should note that many items on this list came from Planned Parenthood's own literature. Sometimes the organization needs to be reminded about the values it proposes.
2. M. Zelnik and Y. Kim, "Sex Education and Its Association with Teenage Sexual Activity, Pregnancy, and Contraceptive Use," *Family Planning Perspectives*, vol. 14, no. 3 (1982), pp. 117-26; Stan E. Weed and Joseph Olsen, "Policy and Program Considerations for Teenage Pregnancy Prevention: A Summary for Policymakers," *Family Perspectives*, vol. 22, no. 3 (1989), pp. 235-252; Dinah Richard, PhD., "Teenage Pregnancy and Sex Education in the Schools: What Works and What Does Not Work," The San Antonio Crisis Pregnancy Centers (1989), P.O. Box 792011, San Antonio, TX 78279-2011.
3. Weed and Olsen, "Policy and Program Considerations."

Chapter 11

1. Sandra Schoenholtz, Harvey Horowitz, Ronny Shatarkshall, "Sex Education for Emotionally Disturbed Adolescents," *Journal of Youth and Adolescence*, vol. 18, no. 1 (February 1989), pp. 97-106; Carla Thornton, "Needs in Sexuality Education for Children and Adolescents with Physical Disabilities," *Siecus Report*, vol. 9, no. 516 (May/June 1981), p. 1.
2. Jane Douglas, "Health, Sex, and Hygiene in Special Education," *Journal of Visual Impairment and Blindness*, vol. 83, no. 2 (February 1989), pp. 125-26.

Chapter 12

1. Roberta A. Hibbard, M.D., and Donald P. Orr, M.D., "Incest and Sexual Abuse," *Seminars in Adolescent Medicine*, vol. 1, no. 3 (1985), pp. 23-29.

2. Ibid.
3. Allie C. Kilpatrick, "Some Correlates of Women's Childhood Sexual Experiences: A Retrospective Study," *Journal of Sex Research*, vol. 22, no. 2 (May 1986), pp. 221-41.
4. Ibid, p. 240.
5. "Child Abuse Can Often Lead to Adult Gynecological Problems," *Ob-Gyn News*, July 1-14, 1990, p. 2.
6. "Women Under Assault," *Newsweek* (July 16, 1990), p. 23.
7. Daniel G. Linz, Edward Donnerstein, and Steven Penrod, "Effects of Long-term Exposure to Violent and Sexually Degrading Depictions of Women," *Journal of Personality and Social Psychology*, vol. 55, no. 5 (November 1988), p. 759.
8. Luis T. Garcia, "Exposure to Pornography and Attitudes about Women and Rape: A Correlational Study," *Journal of Sex Research*, vol. 22, no. 3 (August 1986), p. 383.
9. John M. Leventhal, M.D., "Have There Been Changes in the Epidemiology of Sexual Abuse of Children during the 20th Century?" *Pediatrics*, vol. 82, no. 5 (November 1988), p. 773.

Chapter 13
1. Herant Katchadourian and Donald T. Lunde, *Fundamentals of Human Sexuality*, second ed. (New York: Holt, Rinehart and Winston, 1975), p. 216.
2. Elizabeth Moberly has taken a new look at research on homosexuality and come up with some interventions for the church. She has written *Homosexuality: A New Christian Ethic*.
3. Barbara Johnson, mother of a formerly gay son and founder of Spatula Ministry, has written several books and sends out a cheery monthly newsletter. Contact: Spatula Ministry, Box 444, La Habra, CA 90631, (213) 691-7369.
4. Exodus International is a clearinghouse for programs and activities that are available for homosexuals who wish to leave the lifestyle of homosexuals. Contact: Exodus International, P.O. Box 2121, San Rafael, CA 94912, (415) 454-1017.
5. Mary S. Calderone, "Children and Parents as Sexual People," *Health Education* (November/December 1982), p. 48.
6. Philip Sarrel and Lorna Sarrel, "Beyond the Birds and the Bees: Talking to Children about Sex," *Redbook* (October 1981), p. 47.
7. Chuck Swindoll, *Sanctity of Life* (Dallas: Word Publishing, 1990).
8. "Position Papers on Reproductive Health Care for Adolescents," *Journal of American Health Care*, vol. 4, no. 3 (1983), p. 206.
9. "The Games Teenagers Play," *Newsweek* (September 1, 1980), p. 48.

Bibliography

Bardwidk, Judith M. *Psychology of Women*. New York: Harper & Row, 1971.

Beach, Waldo, and Niebuhr, Richard H. *Christian Ethics*. 2nd ed. New York: The Ronald Press Company, 1973.

Bennett, William J. "Teaching the Young About Sex." *Education Digest* (April 1981): 33-35.

Blitchington, W. Peter. *Sex Roles and the Christian Family*. Wheaton, IL: Tyndale House, 1971.

Buth, Lenore. *Sexuality: God's Precious Gift to Parents and Children*. St. Louis: Concordia, 1982.

Calderone, Mary S. "Children and Parents as Sexual People." Health Education (November-December 1982): 42-48.

_____. "Why Parents Can't Say Enough About Sex." *U.S. Catholic* (October 1982): 26-32.

Calderone, Mary S., and Johnson, Eric W. *The Family Book about Sexuality*. New York: Harper & Row, 1981.

Calderone, Mary S., and Ramey, James W. *Talking with Your Child about Sex*. New York: Random House, 1982.

Campbell, Ross. *How to Really Love Your Teenager*. Wheaton, IL: Victor Books, 1981.

Chamberlin, Leslie J. "Sex and Today's Children." *Clearing House*, vol. 54 (May 1981): 414-17.

"Child Abuse Can Often Lead to Adult Gynecological Problems." *Ob-Gyn News* (July 1-14, 1990): 2.

Christenson, Reo M. "How to Put Premarital Sex on Hold: A Primer for Parents." *Christianity Today* (February 19, 1982): 16-19.

Comer, James. "Speaking of Sex." *Parents* (December 1982): 100.

Corsini, Raymond, ed. *Current Psychotherapies*. Itasco, IL: F. E. Peacock Publishers, 1973.

Crenshaw, Theresa L., and Crenshaw, Roger T. *Concepts of Effective Sex Therapy*. Seminar materials, 1978.

_____. *Expressing Your Feelings*. San Diego: Theresa Crenshaw, 1982.

Darling, Carol A., and Hicks, Mary W. "Parental Influence on Adolescent Sexuality: Implications for Parents and Educators." *Journal of Youth and Adolescence*, vol. 11 (June 1982): 231-45.

Dillow, Joseph C. *Solomon on Sex*. Nashville: Thomas Nelson, 1977.

Douglas, Jane, "Health, Sex, and Hygiene in Special Education." *Journal of Visual Impairment and Blindness*, vol. 83, no. 2 (February 1989): 125-26

Durden-Smith, Jo, and DiSimone, Diane. *Sex and the Brain*. New York: Arbor House, 1983.

Earle, John R., and Perricone, Philip J. "Premarital Sexuality: A Ten-Year Study of Attitudes and Behavior on a Small University Campus." *The Journal of Sex Research*, vol. 22, no. 3 (August 1986): 304-10.

"Family Sexuality More than 'Birds and Bees.'" *USA Today*, vol. 109 (February 1981): 7-8.

Forliti, John E. "Teaching Sexuality, Confidence is the Key." *Momentum*, vol. 13 (May 1982): 33-35.

Fox, Greer Litton. "The Mother-Adolescent Daughter Relationship as a Sexual Socialization Structure: A Research Review." *Family Relations* (January 1980): 21-27.

"The Games Teen-Agers Play." *Newsweek* (September 1, 1980): 48-53.

Garcia Luis T. "Exposure to Pornography and Attitudes about Women and Rape: A Correlational Study." *Journal of Sex Research*, vol. 22, no. 3 (August 1986): 382.

Gardner-Loulan, Jo Ann; Lopez, Bonnie; and Quackenbush, Marcia. *Period*. San Francisco: New Glide Publications, 1979.

Gordon, Sol, and Gordon, Judith. *Raising a Child Conservatively in a Sexually Permissive World*. New York: Simon and Schuster, 1983.

_____. "When and How to Talk to Your Children About Sex." *McCall's* (September 1983): 14, 19, 124.

Heiman, Julia; LoPiccolo, Leslie; and LoPiccolo, Joseph. *Becoming Orgasmic: A Sexual Growth Program for Women*. Englewood Cliffs, NJ: Prentice-Hall, 1976.

Hibbard, Roberta A., M.D., and Orr, Donald P., M.D. "Incest and Sexual Abuse." Seminars in Adolescent Medicine, vol. 1, no. 3 (1985): 23-29.

Horner, Tom. *Sex in the Bible*. Rutland, VT.: Charles E. Tuttle, 1974.

Ilg, Francis L., and Ames, Louise Bates. *The Gesell Institute's Child Behavior*. New York: Harper & Row, 1955.

Johnson, Rex. "Talking to Teens about Sex." *Virtue* (July-August 1982): 42-45.

Joy, Donald. *Bonding*. Word, Inc., 1985.

___. *Re-Bonding,* Word, Inc., 1986.

Juhasz, Anne McCreary. "Sex Education: Today's Myth—Tomorrow's Reality." *Health Education* (January-February 1983): 16-18.

Juhasz, Anne McCreary, and Sonnenshein-Schneider, Mary. "Adolescent Sexuality: Values, Morality and Decision Making." *Adolescence,* vol. 22, no. 87 (Fall 1987): 589.

Kantner, J. F., and Zelnik, M. "Sexual Experiences of Young Unmarried Women in the U.S." *Family Planning Perspectives*, vol. 4 (1972): 9-18.

Katchadourian, Herant, and Lunde, Donald T. *Fundamentals of Human Sexuality.* 2nd ed. New York: Holt, Rinehart and Winston, 1975.

Katz, Lilian G. "Where Did I Come From? *Parents* (September 1981): 102.

Ketterman, Grace H. *How to Teach Your Child about Sex.* Old Tappan, NJ: Fleming H. Revell, 1981.

Kilpatrick, Allie C. "Some Correlates of Women's Childhood Sexual Experiences: A Retrospective Study." *Journal of Sex Research*, vol. 22, no. 2 (May 1986): 239.

Kirby, Douglas. "The Effects of School Sex Education Programs: A Review of the Literature." *IT Journal of School Health* (December 1980): 559-63.

Koblinsky, Sally A. *Sexuality Education for Parents of Young Children: A Facilitator Training Manual.* Fayetteville, NY: Ed-U-Press, 1983.

Koblinsky, Sally, and Atkinson, Jean. "Parental Plans for Children's Sex Education. *Family Relations* (January 1982): 29-35.

Leventhal, John M., M.D. "Have There Been Changes in the Epidemiology of Sexual Abuse of Children During the 20th Century?" *Pediatrics*, vol. 82, no. 5 (November 1988): 773.

Lewinsohn, Richard. *A History of Sexual Customs.* New York: Harper & Row, 1971.

Lewis, Howard R., and Lewis, Martha E. "How to Talk with Teenagers about Virginity." *Families* (November 1981): 68-74.

Linz, Daniel G.; Donnerstein, Edward; and Penrod, Steven. "Effects of Long-term Exposure to Violent and Sexually Degrading Depictions of Women." *Journal of Personality and Social Psychology*, vol. 55, no. 5 (November 1988): 759.

Livingston, Carole. *Why Was I Adopted?* Secaucus, NJ: Lyle Stuart, 1978.

McNab, Warren L. "Advocating Elementary Sex Education." *Health Education* (September-October 1981): 22-25.

Marcello, Michael. "Sex Education Books: A Historical Sampling in the Literature." *Children's Literature in Education*, vol. 13 (Fall 1982): 138-49.

Miles, Herbert J. *Sexual Understanding before Marriage.* Grand Rapids: Zondervan, 1971.

Moberly, Elizabeth. *Homosexuality: A New Christian Ethic.* Attic Press, Rt. 2, Stony Point, Greenwood, SC 29646; 1983.

"Neilsen Report Gets the Picture on Generation Gap." *L.A. Times.* (June 11, 1990).

Penner, Clifford, and Penner, Joyce. *The Gift of Sex.* Waco, TX.: Word Books, 1981.

Phipps, William E. "Masturbation: Vice or Virtue?" *Journal of Religion and Health*, vol. 16 (1977): 183-95.

Pomeranz, Virginia E., and Schultz, Dodi. "When Sex Rears Its Curious Head." *Parents* (August 1983): 88.

Pomeroy, Wardell. *Boys and Sex.* New York: Dell, 1968.

————. *Girls and Sex.* New York: Dell, 1968.

————. *Your Child and Sex.* New York: Dell, 1974.

"Position Papers on Reproductive Health Care for Adolescents." *Journal of Adolescent Health Care*, vol. 4, no. 3 (1983): 206.

Rekers, George Alan. *Shaping Your Child's Sexual Identity.* Grand Rapids: Baker Book House, 1982.

Richards, Dinah. "Teenage Pregnancy and Sex Education in the Schools: What Works and What Does Not Work." The San Antonio Crisis Pregnancy Centers, 1989; P.O. Box 792011, San Antonio, TX 78279-2011.

Roberts, Francis. "Whatever Became of the Latency Period?" *Parents* (September 1980).

Safran, C. "Why Religious Women Are Good Lovers," *Redbook*, vol. 146, no. 103 (April 1976): 103, 155-56, 158-59.

Sarrel, Philip, and Sarrel, Lorna. "Beyond the Birds and the Bees: Talking to Children about Sex." *Redbook* (October 1981): 42-48.

Scales, Peter. "Sexuality Education: The Value of Values." *Planned Parenthood, Emphasis Subscriber Services,* 810 Seventh Avenue, New York, NY 10019.

Scanzoni, Letha Dawson. *Sex Is a Parent Affair.* Toronto: Bantam Books, 1983.

"Sex Ed 101 for Kids and Parents." *Newsweek* (September 1, 1980).

"Sexual Attitudes in Films for the Youth Market." *Sexual Medicine Today* (October 1982): 26-32.

Shapiro, Laura. "Guns and Dolls." *Newsweek* (May 28, 1990): 56-65.

Schoenholtz, Sandra; Horowitz, Harvey; Shatarkshall, Ronny. "Sex Education for Emotionally Disturbed Adolescents." *Journal of Youth and Adolescence*, vol. 18, no. 1 (February 1989): 97-106.

Shedd, Charlie W. *The Stork Is Dead.* New York: Pillar Books, 1976.

Shirreffs, Janet H., and Dezelsky, Thomas L. "Adolescent Perceptions of Sex Ed Needs: 1972-1978. *Journal of School Health*, vol. 49 (June 1979): 343-46.

Smedes, Lewis B. *Sex for Christians.* Grand Rapids: William B. Eerdmans, 1981.

Smith, Harold Ivan. *A Part of Me Is Missing.* Eugene, OR: Harvest House, 1979.

Smith, Virginia Watts. *The Single Parent.* Old Tappan, NJ: Fleming H. Revell, 1976.

Stolk, Mary Van. "Sexual Information: Birthright of the Child." *Childhood Education* (September 1980): 34-35.

Strick, Lisa Wilson. "How to Talk to Your Child about Sex." *Woman's Day* (October 4, 1983): 38-40, 47.

Strom, Kay Marshall. *Chosen Families.* Grand Rapids: Zondervan, 1985.

Studer, Marlena, and Thornton, Arland. "Adolescent Religiosity and Contraceptive Usage." *Journal of Marriage and the Family*, vol. 49, no. 1 (February 1987): 122.

Swindoll, Chuck. *Sanctity of Life*, Dallas: Word Publishing, 1990.

"This Is What You Thought about Teen Sex and Parents." *Glamour*, vol. 80 (August 1982): 27.

Thompson, Elizabeth. "Socialization for Sexual Contraceptive Behavior: Moral Absolutes Versus Relative Consequences." *Youth and Society*, vol. 14 (September 1982): 103, 128.

Thornburg, Hershel D. "Adolescent Sources of Information on Sex." *Journal of School Health*, vol. 51 (April 1981): 274-77.

Thornton, Carla. "Needs in Sexuality Education for Children and Adolescents with Physical Disabilities." *Siecus Report*, vol. 9, no. 516 (May-June 1981): 1.

Wallach, Michael A., and Wallach, Lisa. *Psychology's Sanction for Selfishness.* San Francisco: W. H. Freeman, 1983.

Walters, Ronald G. Walters. *Primers for Prudery: Sexual Advice to Victorian America.* Englewood Cliffs, NJ: Prentice-Hall, 1974: 1-2.

Weed, Stan E., and Olsen, Joseph. "Policy and Program Considerations for Teenage Pregnancy Prevention: A Summary for Policymakers." *Family Perspectives*, vol. 22, no. 3, (1989): 235-52.

Wessler, Martin. *Christian View of Sex Education.* St. Louis: Concordia, 1968.

Wilder, Rachel. "Are Sexual Standards Inherited?" *Science Digest*, vol. 90 (July 1982): 69.

"Women Under Assault," *Newsweek* (July 16, 1990): 23.

Yates, Alayne. *Sex without Shame.* New York: William Morrow, 1978.

Zelnik, M., and Kim, Y. "Sex Education and Its Association with Teenage Sexual Activity, Pregnancy, and Contraceptive Use," *Family Planning Perspectives*, vol. 14, no. 3 (1982): 117-26.

Zilbergeld, Bernie. *Male Sexuality.* New York: Bantam Books, 1978.

Other Good Harvest House Reading

TOO OLD, TOO SOON
by *Doug Fields*

Kids today are on the express lane to adulthood, and they need all the help parents can give them to negotiate the hazards. Youth pastor and author Doug Fields helps parents evaluate the critical part they play in assuring that their kids develop character as well as talents in our success-driven society.

BEST FRIENDS FOR LIFE
by *V. Gilbert Beers*

Nothing is more important for children than having parents who share their hearts. V. Gilbert Beers, father of five and bestselling author, shares how to reach the child's heart and how to develop the kind of *talking relationship* with your children that will bring a lifelong friendship.

TEENAGERS: PARENTAL GUIDANCE SUGGESTED
by *Rich Wilkerson*

With dynamic impact, well-known youth speaker Rich Wilkerson has captured for every sincere parent the secrets of achieving a fulfilling relationship with his or her teen. Honest answers for the tough issues we face with our children. Formerly entitled *Hold Me While You Let Me Go*.

SUCCESSFUL SINGLE PARENTING
by *Gary Richmond*

Author Gary Richmond offers practical help and suggestions to single parents in this valuable guide to successful single parenting. *Successful Single Parenting* provides answers to the toughest questions single parents face. Here is a resource of information and encouragement that parents can turn to again and again.